Daily grace

Daily grace

from Philippians and Colossians

George M. Philip

EVANGELICAL PRESS

RUTHERFORD HOUSE
Encouraging Effective Ministry

EVANGELICAL PRESS
Faverdale North Industrial Estate, Darlington, DL3 0PH,
England

Evangelical Press USA
P. O. Box 825, Webster, New York 14580, USA

e-mail: sales@evangelicalpress.org
web: www.evangelicalpress.org

RUTHERFORD HOUSE
17 Claremont Park, Edinburgh, EH6 7PJ, Scotland

First published 2004

British Library Cataloguing in Publication Data available

ISBN 0 85234 560 7

Printed and bound in Great Britain by Creative Print and
Design Wales, Ebbw Vale, South Wales.

To Joy

my wife and partner in God's work

Paul's letter to the Philippians

Introduction

This is one of Paul's most personal letters, so full of detail that it has to be studied almost verse by verse. Paul himself speaks of repetition (3:1) and we will not hesitate to spend more than one daily reading on certain passages. He tells us a great deal about himself, his feelings and his experiences. He gives instruction about Christian service and encouragement to believers in difficult situations.

The letter was written from prison (1:13), but from which prison and for what reason he was imprisoned we are not sure. It may have been Caesarea, Ephesus or Rome, and a full discussion of these possibilities can be found in commentaries such as the *New Bible Commentary* (IVP).

Paul had often been imprisoned for the sake of the gospel (2 Cor. 11:23). In Philippians he explains that his imprisonment was, in the providence of God, a means of furthering the gospel (1:12; cf. Rom. 8:28). He tells the church at Philippi that he is not sure whether the issue would result in release or execution (1:19-22). Later on, in prison in Rome, he knew the end of his life and ministry was very near (2 Tim. 4:6-8).

We need to remember that Paul's imprisonments were not always brief spells of custody. Acts 24:24-27 refers to a spell of two years, and Acts 28:17-20,30-31 also mentions a period of two years of what was either limited custody with some freedom of movement or an 'open' prison with no restriction on visitors. Furthermore, while imprisoned in Philippi he experienced physical suffering, the tremendous upheaval of an earthquake, glorious conversions and the humbling of unjust magistrates (see Acts 16:19-40).

The writer

Read also Acts 15:35 - 16:10

It is good to set the narrative in its historical setting before starting to study the epistle in detail. The story of the founding of the church at Philippi is recorded in the Acts of the Apostles. It took place at the beginning of Paul's second missionary journey. Barnabas and Paul, two great men chosen by God, had already completed one missionary tour, which is described in Acts chapters 13-14. After a spell of continuing ministry in their home church at Antioch a further missionary journey was planned. Barnabas wanted his nephew Mark on the team but Paul objected because the young man had deserted them on the earlier journey (Acts 13:13). There was a deep disagreement between the two great men (Acts 15:35-41) and they went their separate ways. Paul recruited Silas and set off with the blessing of the church (Acts 15:40). However convinced Paul was about the stand he took, there must have been a costly ache in his heart over the breakdown of fellowship with Barnabas who had a great regard for him.

After a spell of ministry during which he recruited Timothy (Acts 15:41 - 16:5), Paul looked to God for further guidance but nothing seemed to work out (Acts 16:6-8). Whatever way he tried to turn he was blocked by God. Try to imagine Paul's thoughts and feelings, wondering if he had been disobedient to God and so could not see or sense his guiding hand. Had he grieved the Spirit because of his dealings with Barnabas?

Then, just when everything seemed black and hopeless, there came the vision and the call to Macedonia (Acts 16:9-12), to which he responded with glad and eager assurance.

The city

Read also Acts 16:11-15

Paul would have good knowledge of the area he was moving into. He would have been aware of Greek culture, drama, literature, architecture and philosophy, together with the achievements of Roman law, government and trade. It was from such a context of human achievement that the heart-rending appeal came: 'Come over and help us.' Philippi was the chief city of Macedonia, although Thessalonica was the actual capital. It was a proud city with Roman status. Paul would know the secular atmosphere, materialism, idolatry and the incursion of demonic influence into the life and trade of the people. What did he expect as he went forward in obedience to God's will for him to preach the gospel?

There was no welcoming party, no evangelistic committee, no programme of meetings planned and publicized. But there was the grace of God that always goes before, preparing the ground for the sowing of the seed of the Word.

There was a group of women in a meeting for prayer. They were religious but not believers, in the Christian sense. They had not heard the gospel but seeking hearts were prepared by God for its arrival. There were no men in the group. There does not seem to have been a synagogue in the city, which would have been Paul's normal starting point. No doubt he made enquiries about things pertaining to God and heard about the women. The great missionary was not too proud to sit down and teach at a women's meeting and, as he taught, God opened Lydia's heart so that she believed. Her home then became Paul's base of operations.

A church founded

Read also Acts 16:16-40

The story goes on to tell of men making money through a sorcerer girl who was eventually delivered by Christ's power. Then there was the uproar incited because of loss of profit, and the beatings, prison, earthquake and the tough jailer's conversion. Paul now knew why God had sent him to Philippi, but it was not long before he and his companions were sent away by the authorities.

However, by that time there was a group of believers meeting in Lydia's house. Its members included three very different people: Lydia herself, the wealthy businesswoman; the one-time sorcerer girl; and the rough prison jailer. There would have been others who had gathered both before and after Paul's departure, and they must have been thrilled and encouraged when Paul, in his letter, addressed them as 'saints in Christ Jesus'.

The word 'saint' signifies someone separated from the rest of society and set apart for God, through faith in Jesus Christ. This group of saints lived in the city of Philippi but, having been set apart by the saving grace of God, they belonged to God's heavenly city (Phil. 3:20). This was their true identity and destiny, both personally and as a church. They were gathered together in an identifiable company. All were included. Even the most 'ordinary' believer was God's man or woman, including those who had only recently been converted to Christ. They were one in fellowship and service with the elders and deacons who, no doubt, had been appointed by Paul and Timothy before they left (cf. Acts 14:21-23).

Amazing grace

Read also Ephesians 1:3-8

Paul's opening greeting is full of encouragement and instruction. Notice first how he and Timothy are described. There is no emphasis on rank or importance, even though Paul was aware, as is plain from his other letters, that he was a chosen man, called to be an apostle (Rom. 1:1; 1 Cor. 15:7-9; Acts 26:16-18).

Here there was no need to emphasize authority, because these Christians held him and his ministry in high regard. Right through his life Paul regarded himself as a servant, a bondservant (NKJV) of Jesus Christ. His personal rights and privileges had no real place in his thoughts. He was a man mastered by Jesus Christ. He regarded himself as greatly privileged (Eph. 3:8), entrusted with the stewardship of God's gospel (1 Cor. 4:1-2), and his supreme desire was to be found faithful right to the end of his life (Acts 20:17-24).

The greeting or benediction in verse 2 would in itself encourage and bless the disciples in Philippi. It is the grace of God that brings salvation (Titus 2:11). It is all-sufficient grace (2 Cor. 12:9), abounding grace (Rom. 5:20, AV), never-ending grace (John 1:16), rich grace lavished upon us (Eph. 1:3-8). By God's grace we have access into God's presence, right to his throne (Heb. 4:16). As J. I. Packer says, in his book *Knowing God*, 'Grace is **G**od's **R**iches **A**t **C**hrist's **E**xpense'.[1]

Along with grace there is peace: peace with God, peace from God and the peace of God, which Paul will speak of later, in chapter 4.

Encouragers

Read also 2 Timothy 1:15-18; 4:9-18

Paul's heart of love for this people is obvious. But it is not enough to *feel* love for people, nor even to *pray* for them. Love should be *expressed* in words, whether face to face or in a letter. Imagine the encouragement it must have been to the Christians to hear these words read to the gathered company. When Paul thought about these believers he was encouraged in his own spirit and in his work for God. Do we realize the effect our faithfulness, or even our lack of it, can have on others?

Some Christians cause heartbreak to their ministers but some, because of their love and dependability, are a means of grace. Some can always be counted on to be in their place, especially for prayer. Many can look back over years and are encouraged by remembering those whose prayers touched the heart, whose lives had the marks of Christ, and who stood firm through hard and costly times. Speaking together and recalling past days encourages us to go on in faithful service (Mal. 3:16).

Paul was never slow to express his gratitude to those who had worked with him and encouraged him even when some were not behaving as they should (Phil. 4:2-3). At other times he speaks movingly of some whose loyalty to himself as well as to the work cost them dearly (Rom. 16:3-4). Their devotion would have inspired Paul to try to be worthy of them. He knew the importance of the ministry of encouragement.

Partnership in service

Read also Matthew 26:36-46

True Christian fellowship is found, maintained and en-
riched in the twofold context of prayer and service in the
gospel. In our unqualified commitment in these areas we
are brought into God's presence and we are kept there. In
that way we are delivered from preoccupation with ourselves and are made aware that there are issues of far greater
importance than our own needs, fulfilment and happiness.
Paul will expound this theme in detail in chapter 3. Here
he is simply opening his heart in gratitude to God and to
the believers in Philippi, all of whom were younger in the
faith than Paul himself, many having been converted under
his ministry.

On hearing Paul's words read from the letter, you can
imagine the people saying, 'Paul, we do pray for you.' That
is part of the reason for Paul's thanksgiving to God. It is so
easy to say to people that we will pray for them and then
very soon grow weary in the task. There are ministers and
missionaries who thank God for those in their home
churches who have continued to pray for them down
through the years from the day they were commissioned to
service in the gospel. This is the partnership that Paul gives
thanks for. It is not just fellowship, sweet and blessed as
that is. It is in every sense a working partnership: working
together with God (1 Cor. 3:9; 2 Cor. 6:1). Think of it as
being 'in the same team' as God, side by side with him.
This is the thrill of Christian service. When we work together bonds are forged which last and can deepen, even
though as time passes we may have only brief and infre-
quent meetings. The truth is that we meet regularly and
significantly at God's mercy-seat when we pray for one
another.

Confidence in God

Read also Jeremiah 18:1-6

Read again from verse 3 and see that while Paul's first encouragement in service is partnership in prayer, the second great encouragement is confidence in God. In expressing his own confidence in the one whom he has proved in so many ways, Paul gives a message of assurance to his fellow believers. After all, some of them were recent converts with so much to learn and so much to cope with as they lived and worked in a godless society.

We all need to grasp the fact that it was God who began the good work of salvation in our lives. Read Ephesians 2:1-5 and emphasize the words 'But ... God'. It was God, by his Holy Spirit, who brought us under the sound of the gospel, opening our eyes and hearts to our need of a Saviour, and enabling us to believe. It was God who showered his redeeming love on us, making us his children. He gave us new life in Christ, with the purpose of moulding and transforming our personalities and lives into the likeness of his Son (1 John 3:1-3).

God has his perfect plan for all that he will do for us, in us and through us in life and service (Jer. 29:11). In the ongoing process there will no doubt be many mistakes, failures and rebellions on our part, but even then God is not deterred. He made plain through Jeremiah that when the vessel of our lives is marred, the great Potter immediately sets about remaking the vessel to make it fit for his service. It is wonderful when we see the beginnings of change in the lives of believers and the first hints of spiritual potential. God works on. His objective is that in due time he will see the travail of his soul and be satisfied (Isa. 53:11, AV).

On with God

Read also Ephesians 3:14-21

We need to remind ourselves again of the assurance of verse 6 as it applies to our personal lives, to the local work of which we are a part, and to the worldwide historical development of the work of the gospel. Consider how in the Lord's Prayer we pray that God's kingdom will come. That is not just a pious hope, even though some say the words as if they had little confidence in it happening. At the end of that prayer (although the words are relegated to a footnote in most modern translations) the affirmation is made, 'Thine is the kingdom'. The kingdom, the power to bring it to pass, and the glory all belong to God alone. But we are given the privilege of sharing in the work, taking up where others have worked before us, and then passing it on to the next generation (John 4:37-38). There is no doubt as to the issue. It is Christ who builds his church and the gates of hell shall not prevail (Matt. 16:18). The gates of hell, the powers of evil in the world, are the ones on the defensive, *not* the church of Jesus Christ! we have all the power we need

Do we still sing 'Onward Christian Soldiers' or do we no longer believe in spiritual warfare as Paul speaks of it in Ephesians 6:10-18? All through the Bible the people of God are urged to go on and to go forward because there is territory in the world and in human lives to be claimed, fought for and won for Christ. Have we begun to grasp what God has graciously planned and prepared for us and for our lives (1 Cor. 2:9)? He is able to do far above all we ask or think (Eph. 3:14-21). In the context of all the battles and struggles, in spite of them and indeed through them, God's grace is at work. May the truth of the doxology in Jude 24-25 thrill our hearts!

Sharing

Read also 2 Corinthians 4:7-12

Paul, the great missionary theologian, was a man of commitment, drive and determination, ready to lose everything for Christ's sake. When necessary, he would risk losing valued friends because of loyalty to the gospel (Gal. 2:11-14). But he is seen here to be a man of wonderful tenderness and sensitivity. He cared for his people, and he told them so. Those he ministered to, he carried in his heart. Of course, no man can ever preach truly unless he sees his congregation as precious to God, as men and women who are of great value, and who have to be shepherded and fed (John 21:15-17).

If we become impatient with people, we need to remember just how patient and forbearing God has been with us. Why are we so slow to express love and care, especially for the people entrusted to us? Is it because we do not really pray for them? The manly Jesus often spoke with tenderness (John 14:18). God the Father did the same. His Word was made flesh, and expressed in human terms (John 1:14).

Paul is deeply moved when he thinks of those loving, loyal folk sharing with him not only the joys of the gospel but also the criticism, prejudice and rejection. Remember how Jesus spoke of those who had continued with him in his trials (Luke 22:28). Paul reminds the Philippians that they are bound up together with him in his battles for the ongoing worldwide preaching of the gospel. When *we* are battling in faith, the fruit of the struggle and victory may be being worked out in the situations of missionaries we pray for. What a privilege!

A short prayer

Read also 2 Peter 1:3-9

In verse 7 Paul has spoken of the defence of the gospel, in answering prejudice and correcting misrepresentations so that the truth will stand clear. He has also spoken of the confirmation of the gospel, preaching, teaching, applying, exhorting and challenging, which was the pattern of his whole ministry, as he *reasoned* out of the Scriptures (Acts 17:2-3; 18:1-4). Paul did not argue. That can so easily become ill-tempered, and elsewhere he warns against the kind of disputing that is both unproductive and a distraction (1 Tim. 1:3-7; 6:3-5).

In verse 8 he speaks of the particular affection and love that grows between those who have fought and worked side by side in Christ's service. Remember that these were some of his first converts in Europe and he must have been thrilled by how they had stood firm and grown in their faith. This is what inspires his prayer: a short prayer in terms of the words used, but with amazing depth and comprehensiveness. He prays for their spiritual growth and this will be the evidence that spiritual life has been born in them. After all, if we are born of God (John 1:13), then that life *must* and *will* grow, and will manifest itself in our human lives. Paul prays that their love might grow: their love for God, for the gospel and for others. Their love must grow from the first thrill of excitement in their conversion to a deepening, more settled trust, commitment and loyalty. This is how genuine human relationships develop and it should be the same in spiritual life. No Christian can live and go on with Christ on the basis of repeated surges of 'excitement'. Love is much more basic, stable and lasting.

Learn what God is like

Read also Isaiah 40:9-11,27-31

True love is not blind. It is grounded in truth. That is why
Paul prays for an increasing knowledge: learning what God
is like, so that trust grows. It is from trust in God that we go
on to serve, no matter how circumstances develop. It is as
we know God that prayer becomes more and more a natural part of our lives. Instinctively we take everything to
God in prayer, especially when we do not understand what
is happening, because we are persuaded that God knows
exactly what he is doing with us and we trust, even in the
dark (Job 23:8-10).

As we learn of God there should come a spirit of discernment, a sense of what has real value, so that we will
not be deceived by what is false and cheap. This discernment is accompanied by a sense of tact or perception, so
that we make true judgements rather than simply reacting
to our feelings. Paul wants the Christians to have a grasp of
what is vital so that they will know when to stand firm and
refuse to give ground, and when to yield graciously because no real issue of principle is involved. There is an apt
prayer asking God to grant us the serenity to accept what
cannot be changed, the courage to change what can be
changed, and the wisdom to know the difference.[2] The picture we are being given is that of an increasingly mature
and balanced life, which is a reflection and expression of
the life of Jesus. It is the kind of human life that is attractive and draws people to think of God. It is 'natural' because
it is truly 'spiritual'. It is not a lifestyle adopted for occasions
of witnessing or service. It is free from extremes. It is a life
that has the mark of peace. However, because it is Jesus'
life in us and expressed through us, it will annoy and even
enrage some people (John 15:18-25).

The fruit of the Spirit

Read also Galatians 5:16-25

Paul says three further things about the life that Christians should live. It must be pure in its inner character and blameless in outward behaviour. It is a life without fatal, hidden cracks; it is lived out in the open with God. It is 'walking in the light', or walking out in the open with God, with nothing to hide (1 John 1:5-7). It is the kind of life we will not be ashamed of on the day of Christ, when he comes in his glory and we stand before him (1 John 2:28). This life will be filled with, not just touched or marked by, the fruit of righteousness, which comes through Christ by the Holy Spirit. In the searching passage of Galatians 5:16-25, the nine-fold fruit of the Spirit sets a tremendous challenge because all these graces belong together, stemming from love. This is the work and the great objective of God's Spirit in our hearts and lives. As the hymn-writer says, 'And every virtue we possess, and every victory won, and every thought of holiness are His alone.'[3] The objective of this life from beginning to end and in every situation is that it should bring glory and praise to God. We need to pause, and to pray along the lines of these words from the hymn by Edwin Hatch (1835-89).

Breathe on me, Breath of God;
Fill me with life anew,
That I may love what Thou dost love,
And do what Thou wouldst do.

Breathe on me, Breath of God,
Until my heart is pure,
Until with Thee I will one will,
To do and to endure.

God's sure providence

Read also Proverbs 3:1-7

The Philippians had heard of Paul's imprisonment and he makes use of this to teach an important lesson. He has already spoken of encouragement in God and partnership with God, and now he emphasizes the need for confidence in God. He is aware of the overruling power of God in his sovereign providence. No doubt the believers were praying that Paul might be delivered from prison. He assures them that their prayers are being answered, not in the way they asked or expected, but in a way that was more wonderful.

We sometimes sing that God moves in a mysterious way, and Scripture confirms that his ways are past finding out (Rom. 11:33). But we must not forget that the objective of God's activities is to carry out his good and perfect will. Paul tells the Philippians, his prayer partners, that it is amazing what God has done and how he has done it. Paul's arrest had led to an evangelist operating within the central offices of Roman government. Christ and the gospel were general subjects of conversation among Christians and non-Christians alike. The presence of Paul and the openings for witness that this had created had encouraged the Christians to be bolder in witnessing to their faith.

Another aspect of how his imprisonment was serving to advance the gospel is that, prevented from continuing his missionary travels and preaching, Paul now had time, opportunity and energy to write some of his epistles to the churches. These verses emphasize the active, overruling providence of God, a fact that we forget when circumstances are hard, or mysterious, or both. Do we really believe Romans 8:28; Ephesians 1:11; and Psalm 31:14-15?

Long-term trust

Read also Genesis 37:23-28; 50:15-20

God's overruling of circumstances in his wise and sure providence is a vital subject. We must learn to believe and to rest in God's providence even when, and especially when, we do not see any signs of his presence and activity. We live by faith not by sight (2 Cor. 5:7) and that means we must go on serving him, coping with adverse circumstances, believing that God is at work and that, in due time if it pleases him, we shall see and understand events. We can all remember times in our own lives when it would have been easy to jump to wrong conclusions and to see only the devil at work and not God.

In Acts 8:1-8, when the work of the gospel was prospering, fierce persecution broke out. It was not a tragedy in spite of the obvious suffering of the believers because, as a result, the fires of revival were scattered far and wide. In Acts 18:1-4, following government persecution in Rome, two people became refugees and moved to the very unpleasant city of Corinth. Then it became evident they had been sent there to be partners with Paul in ministry to the churches. Trace the same good hand of God in the story of Paul's journey to Rome. It was a process that involved ill-treatment, jail, corrupt justice and shipwreck. But God was in it all (Acts 27:21-26) and the story is summarized in the words, 'and *so* we came to Rome' (Acts 28:14).

The same lesson about the long-term providence of God is clear in the story of Joseph and all the wrongs he suffered, some of which were caused by his own overconfidence. In the end he said to his brothers who had treated him so badly, 'You meant evil against me, but God meant it for good' (Gen. 50:20, NKJV). We have a God we can trust.

Despised and rejected

Read also 1 Corinthians 9:1-6,19-23

Paul's attitude is positive and he rejoices for three good reasons. The gospel is being advanced (v. 12), Christ is being proclaimed (v. 18) and Christ is being honoured (v. 20). But his situation was not without hurt and distress. Not all the Christians thought well of Paul. Note that these hurts were not being inflicted by godless unbelievers but by those who believed the gospel and preached Christ. Read Psalm 41:5-9; 55:12-14,20; and John 13:18. There were those who honoured Paul and recognized that his ministry was indeed owned by God. But others disliked him. They had reservations about his person, methods and motives. They concluded that his being in prison was evidence that God was finished with him.

Just why they devalued and despised Paul we cannot tell. Perhaps they resented his radical attitude regarding any departure from or compromise of the gospel (Gal. 1:6-9). Perhaps they were jealous of his standing in the churches and of the fruitfulness of his ministry. Some sought deliberately to add to Paul's hurt by the things they said. Others would seek to hurt by silence, simply ignoring him. Of course, there were those who encouraged Paul by saying that they would keep the work going in Philippi, as he would want them to do, and they promised to keep him informed about all developments. In all this Paul was willing to be nothing, even less than nothing, to be a doormat and to be treated as 'the scum of the earth' (1 Cor. 4:13) so long as Christ was preached. He wanted no one to be distracted from Jesus because of the way he was personally ill-treated. How do we react to Christians who hurt us?

Rejoicing and prayer

Read also Ephesians 6:18-20

Paul is determined to rejoice in God. He refuses to let his circumstances steal his joy and confidence. He believes that if God is for him, it does not really matter who is against him (Rom. 8:31). In this one verse he brings into focus an important lesson with regard to the whole of Christian life and service. He declares the positive and creative link between the prayers of God's people and the operating power of the Holy Spirit. This does not mean that our prayers control the Holy Spirit, although some Christians believe and act as if this were so. God's working is always sovereign, but the whole of Scripture testifies that God is pleased to work through human instruments. It has been said that the prayers of the saints are the decrees of God beginning to work. The human and the divine are brought together in terms of cause and effect. What an encouragement to the church to pray, and what a rebuke to the church when it neglects prayer!

In all our praying we are asking and looking to God to act in specific situations. We do not dictate to God what he should do, but we look for the indications that the gracious, mighty, free-moving Spirit of God is doing his work in answer to our prayers. He is the one who does the work: convicting of sin (John 16:7-11); hovering over chaotic situations and bringing order (Gen. 1:2); working deliverance and giving the supply of power or enabling for specific situations. In the New English Bible a footnote states that Judges 6:34 reads literally, 'The Spirit of God clothed itself with Gideon.' Christians at prayer and the working of the Holy Spirit are bound together in this one verse.

Faith's uncertainties

Read also 2 Timothy 1:8-12; 4:6-8

Paul's rejoicing does not mean that he was sure how things would work out. In fact, he seems unsure as to what he really wanted. That is not surprising, because he was human, just as we are. When he speaks of his deliverance, he may be thinking of release from prison, or vindication in the face of criticism, or even his final salvation, which he speaks of so movingly in 2 Timothy 4:6-8. Yet there is one thing he is quite clear about. He wants Christ to be honoured or glorified in his body, in his person, whether by life or death.

Some years ago one of our church members was terminally ill in hospital. Visited by his minister, he said, 'Ask the Prayer Meeting to pray that I will die like a Christian.' You never forget that kind of pastoral visit! When Paul speaks of his eager expectation he seems to be straining forward, looking ahead, running hard for the finishing tape of the Christian race (Heb. 12:1-2). The only thing that really matters to him is Christ. There are no competitors. It is Christ who has given him life; that life belongs to Christ, and it must be lived for Christ and with Christ. When that life has run its course here on earth and Paul dies, that will be his ultimate gain. Paul regarded himself, in all aspects of his life, as completely at the disposal of Christ, his Lord and Master. If there was to be release from prison and a future spell of service in the gospel he would be thrilled, even if that service brought him more pain and suffering. Service was a delight, not a burdensome duty, and suffering for Jesus' sake was a privilege (Acts 5:40-42). We do well to examine our own attitude and commitment to service. Could we be described as willing servants of Jesus?

Escapism or realism

Read also Revelation 22:1-5

Do we anticipate heaven as positively as Paul does when he says that to be with Christ is far better than to be here in this world? When he says he is hard pressed (v. 23, RSV), did he feel his physical and mental capacities were coming to an end? He would not be thinking that heaven signified an end to all spiritual service. We are told that in heaven, portrayed so gloriously in Revelation, God's servants will serve him and will see him face to face (Rev. 22:1-5). Heaven is *not* a consolation prize. Paul says it is far better, and it is strange that Christians do not talk more about heaven. It is even stranger that ministers do not preach more positively about it. But over against his anticipation of glory, Paul reveals his shepherd-heart in verses 22 and 24. His concern was not what was going to happen to himself but who would care for, teach, guard and guide the flock which God had given to him. They were his spiritual children. He had travailed in birth for them (Gal. 4:19; 1 Cor. 4:15), and for them he would gladly give his life in further service.

As he writes he seems to become persuaded that God's plan was that he would be released. In verses 25-26 Paul seems to anticipate a future ministry in which he and they together would recount the story of all God's wonderful works in their lives, the answered prayer, the blessing and privilege of service. As the work went on they would together glory in Christ Jesus. For Paul and for them, Christ would be pre-eminent (Col. 1:18). They would glory only in the cross of Christ (Gal. 6:14). They would echo the words of C. T. Studd, 'If Jesus Christ be God and died for me, then no sacrifice can be too great for me to make for Him.'[4]

Worthy of the gospel

Read also Ephesians 4:1-3,28-32

Paul makes an appeal from his heart. He seems to be saying that, whatever might happen to him or them in days to come, they must see to it that they live lives worthy of the gospel. After all, our lives are the advertisement boards that draw attention to Jesus (Acts 4:13). This kind of appeal is often made by Paul (Rom. 12:1-2; 1 Thess. 4:1-7). In 1 Thessalonians 5:22 the exhortation is expressed in nega-tive terms. The AV translation suggests we should keep away from anything that *appears* to be evil, lest we give un-believers opportunity to accuse Christians of hypocrisy. Be good, for the gospel's sake.

The positive aspect of the appeal is expressed in Titus 2:7-10. Our lives should adorn the gospel, not in the sense of dressing it up to make it attractive to unbelievers, but in the way that a jeweller sets his precious wares on velvet so that they will be seen to their best advantage, their value being made obvious. Our daily lives should be making plain to others the riches of life, and the blessings, benefits and fulfilment that are found in the life of discipleship. What Paul wanted to hear about them was that they were stand-ing firm, rooted and grounded in Christ (Eph. 3:14-19), never moving away from the doctrines of grace and salvation, always ready to give a reason for the faith they held (1 Peter 3:15). It would not be easy to do that in the atmosphere of the city and they would need to be of one mind and one spirit, with personal preferences and inclinations laid aside and made subject to the need of the work of the gospel. This is always a necessary challenge. Remember the way the disciples argued at the Last Supper over who should have first place (Luke 22:14-24).

Sharing the load

Read also Matthew 11:28-30

This call is to stand firm and to strive together for the faith of the gospel. In any team, when one person does not pull his weight, all the others will have to carry the extra burden. If one believer in the fellowship wanders spiritually, he or she cannot do their fair share and this affects others. The striving Paul is referring to is caused by those who oppose the advance of the gospel. The work can at times be very costly and the load must be shared. This involves the sharing of practical as well as spiritual things, and, if people feel they are too spiritual to take their share of the down-to-earth work, there is something wrong. In this context, think of Jesus' words about taking his yoke and learning from him (Matt. 11:28-30). Our Lord may have had in mind the familiar picture of an old and a young ox yoked together, the young one learning its trade from the experienced one. The old ox would curb the excessive, restless energy of the younger partner, but at the same time take more of the heavy weight of the plough until the younger animal gained both strength and experience. Frisky young animals have to learn to bear the yoke while they still have the old ones to teach them.

The lesson can be applied to many areas of Christian service. For example, in the prayer meeting, the experienced intercessors should not be selfish, praying at length for all the obvious and immediate needs, leaving the less confident people wondering what is left to pray about. When it is hard to pray, that is when experienced men and women should step in, break the barriers (but not with long prayers) and encourage those who need help so that they also can become true intercessors.

Fear not

Read also John 15:18 - 16:4

The exhortation not to be frightened is given because it is so easy to give way to fear. This is one of the great ploys of the devil. Whether we are faced with criticism, opposition, uncertainty or our own failures, we must not panic. All through the Bible come the commands, 'Fear not', 'Let not your heart be troubled' (Isa. 43:1-5; John 14:1). Remember that the battle is the Lord's (2 Chr. 20:15-17) and therefore the ultimate issue is never in doubt. Remember this when it seems that the enemies of the gospel are in fact succeeding. Do not let fear make you jump to conclusions. The spiritual battle is on a broad, geographical and historical front. It began before we arrived and will continue after we have gone (John 4:34-38). At times the great Commander may make a strategic withdrawal in certain sections. This is not defeat but will work out in the interest of the long-term victory. We must stand firm in the faith, and this will be used by God to accomplish two things. It will first of all be a sign to unbelievers, signifying their destruction, whether they are aware of this or not. Secondly, it will confirm believers in their faith and remind them that their salvation and eternal destiny are sure and secure.

Paul finally reminds the Philippians that, like him, they had been given the privilege of suffering for Jesus' sake. When we are suffering because of faithfulness to God and the gospel, we are in good company. It is the way the Master went, and we must not expect a better deal from the world than he had. Read Jesus' words in Matthew 5:10-12; Paul's words in 1 Corinthians 4:9-13; and Peter's words in 1 Peter 2:20-23.

Jesus first

Read also Mark 10:35-44

In chapter one the name of Christ was mentioned at least eighteen times. This is an indication of how Christ-centred Paul was in his life and service. The fruitfulness and effectiveness of individuals and congregations depend on just how Christ-centred they are. In the congregation at Philippi things were not what they should have been and Paul, though loving them deeply, was not blind to the situation and begins with an appeal regarding their attitudes to each other. He points them to Christ. If we read Romans 15:1-3 we see that even Christ did not please himself. In his perfect humanity he was free from all bias and prejudice, and 'self' did not in any way intrude in his service for the Father. For us, 'self' is an abiding danger and snare. Martin Luther said he was more afraid of the great pope Self than all the other popes in Christendom. Self-interest, self-will, self-centredness, self-indulgence are all ugly aspects of our persons and cause all sorts of complications for others, for the work of God, and for ourselves. 'Self' is cruel to others; it excludes others; it uses others and, most significantly, it draws attention away from Christ. Self disturbs and divides the fellowship of the church and distracts from service.

In beginning to deal with this problem on a pastoral level, Paul seeks to make the Christians think of all that they have received from Christ, unworthy though they had been of the least of his mercies (Gen. 32:10, AV). In verse 1 Paul lists some of these blessings: encouragement, love, fellowship, tenderness and compassion; and it seems that these were the very things the Christians were failing to show each other.

A practical test

Read also Matthew 18:21-35

We cannot be sure what caused the strains and tensions in Philippi. In his commentary Hendriksen asks: 'Did some of the members see too much of each other? Were they getting on each other's nerves? Were some beginning to exaggerate the weaknesses and minimize the virtues of other church members? ... Brothers attacking or even just belittling each other make a sorry spectacle before the world.' Paul begins to challenge these Christians on the basis that if they had received rich blessings from Christ, then their gratitude had to be expressed not only to him, but also to each other. Consider carefully Jesus' words in Matthew 18:21-35 and allow them to search the heart, not least the next time you repeat the Lord's Prayer and say, 'Forgive us our debts as we also have forgiven our debtors.'

Have we found encouragement in Christ in the way he has dealt with us: his patience and forbearing, his repeated forgiveness, his helping us back to our feet and never mocking us because of our failures? Have we been moved by his humble serving as he washed the disciples' feet (John 13:1-5,12-17) when the burden of the cross was already heavy on his spirit?

Because he has been so kind to us when we have fallen, should we not be kind to others and help them when they fall (Gal. 6:1-2)? Can we really be Christians if we are indifferent to the needs of others and insensitive to their hurts and to their longing for a word or act of kindness? Paul the pastor searches our hearts.

Love one another

Read also 1 John 4:7-11,20-21

These verses echo the familiar Benediction that speaks of the grace of the Lord Jesus Christ, the love of God the Father and the fellowship of the Holy Spirit. They remind us of the goodness of God, the understanding kindness and sympathetic feeling of our Saviour Jesus Christ (Heb. 2:14-18; 4:14-16), and the promised presence and ministry of the Holy Spirit, our personal comforter, encourager and enabler. Now, says Paul, if these undeserved blessings have been yours, be like Jesus to other people.

Note the words 'tenderness and compassion'. Paul felt this way about the Philippians and he told them (1:8). This is the kind of love that instinctively draws people in their need, assuring them that there is genuine care and the desire to help in a way that neither tramples on tender feelings nor violates their dignity. Think of the way that all sorts of people with varied needs constantly drew near to Jesus (Matt. 15:29-31; Luke 15:1). This care is what real faith and commitment to sound doctrine should produce in our attitudes to and our dealings with each other, and certainly in our preaching. If Paul could see these graces in the lives of Christians whom he loves, he feels he could cope with all the suffering that came to him in his service. He appeals to them to be like-minded, to be one in attitude and purpose. It is not all that difficult if we keep in mind how much we owe to Jesus, and how precious others are to him. People may be difficult to get on with, be hard to love, and be slow in their response to both love and spiritual teaching. But then the Lord Jesus could say that about all of us, and yet he loved without qualification. He persisted in having hope for us and for our service.

Pride and place

Read also 1 Corinthians 12:14-25

Here is a challenge to human pride in all its aspects and actions! The motives in verse 3 are variously expressed in modern versions as selfishness, selfish ambition and conceit. The AV speaks of 'strife and vainglory', which indicate the presence of tension, angling for position, and pride that makes people think they are better than others. Such attitudes have no place in Christian life and fellowship.

There is wise counsel in Romans 12:3 and a reminder in 1 Corinthians 4:1-7 that all we are and have that is of worth comes from God. If we feel we are gifted, humanly or spiritually, in speech, administration, or personality, then we are qualified to be servants. The last part of verse 3 does not mean that we should always be comparing ourselves unfavourably with other people. That is preoccupation with ourselves and is certainly not humility. Such an attitude tends to make us forget that the value God has set on us is declared in the fact that he gave his Son to die for us. Since that is so, no Christian needs to have an inferiority complex. There is a false humility such as that shown by Uriah Heep (a character in *David Copperfield* by Charles Dickens), who is always speaking of being 'humble'. That is self-centred. Humility is very different from the false modesty that says, 'I'm no use at anything' when that is obviously not true. Humility is essentially not thinking about ourselves because we are genuinely thinking of others. We *all* have gifts of various kinds. Some have gifts that cause them to be in the public eye, a dangerous place, a hothouse for the cultivation of pride. Some have gifts that cause them to be 'backroom' men and women; but where would the work of the church be without them?

Consider Jesus

Read also Hebrews 3:1-2; 12:1-4

When we sing the hymn, 'When I survey the wondrous cross', do we really mean the words, 'And pour contempt on all my pride'? Consider the words of the following hymn:

> May the mind of Christ my Saviour
> Live in me from day to day,
> By His love and power controlling
> All I do and say.[5]

That is the message of this wonderful verse that fixes our attention on the Saviour, whose person and life are our example. The AV makes the verse an individual call: be like Jesus in all you do, in the way you do it, and in your motives. The RSV applies the verse to the congregation, giving the principle for all relationships and activities. The NIV reads, 'Your attitude should be the same as that of Christ Jesus.' We need to cultivate the habit of considering Jesus (Heb. 12:3): in his suffering for the salvation of sinners (Isa. 53:3,7); and in the midst of his agony when he prayed for the forgiveness of those who despised and rejected him (Luke 23:34). Consider Jesus' example of lowly service (John 13), and his quiet trust in his Father when he was being reviled (1 Peter 2:21-23). Consider Jesus the faithful apostle and high priest (Heb. 3:1-2); our great advocate, pleading our cause at God's right hand (1 John 2:1; Rom. 8:31-39), who ever lives to make intercession for us; who delights in his Father's will and work (John 17:1,4,5). This is the Jesus who was among us as one who serves, and whose whole life was to minister to others, not to be ministered to (Mark 10:42-45). This Jesus is our great example and his Spirit abides in our hearts. Our lives should bear the family likeness.

The Servant King

Read also Matthew 20:20-28

This marvellous passage which focuses briefly but com-
prehensively on the person of our Lord Jesus Christ must
be studied in detail verse by verse. But first read the whole
passage, which is in two sections. Verses 6-8 speak of the
Saviour who came down to earth from heaven to die on the
cross. Verses 7-11 speak of his exaltation, his being crowned
as King of Kings and his full, final and inescapable victory.
We are shown the King of Kings who became a servant; the
eternal Son of God who became a true man.

   In his life of service as a man he stood and looked over
the city of Jerusalem and wept with an agonized compassion, as he saw people living and dying in their sins, refusing
every appeal of his love and grace (Luke 13:34-35; 19:41-
44). This is the Jesus who came to his own but they did not
receive him (John 1:11). This is the glorious King and Head
of the church who is portrayed outside the door of the
church, knocking and asking for admission (Rev. 3:20). This
is the Jesus who, having loved his own, loved them to the
end in spite of all their failures, pride, ambition and slow-
ness to learn. As we ponder these profound verses, which
some regard as an early hymn or poem, the throbbing
message comes again and again: 'Let this mind be in you
which was also in Christ Jesus' (2:5, AV). Though he was
rich, for our sakes he became poor, so that we through his
poverty might become rich (2 Cor. 8:9). The nature and work
of the Servant King should move us to worship, as in the
words of Charles Wesley in the hymn 'And can it be?':

> Amazing love! How can it be,
> That Thou, my God, should die for me?

The Eternal Son

Read also John 1:1-5,10-14

The humility of Jesus Christ is demonstrated by contrasting who he is and what he became. He was in very nature God. In every way, inward and outward, his essential nature was God. We must never think of him as *just* a man. He was, before time began, God the eternal Son. In the beginning, before the world was ever called into being, the Word was, and was with God, and the Word was God. All things were made by him (John 1:1-3; Col. 1:15-16). This is the Jesus of the Gospels. He knew who and what he was and where he had come from, as is clear from his prayer in John 17:5. Jesus is the express image of God, and anyone who has seen him has seen the Father (John 14:8-9). It seems from verse 10 that Jesus is his name both in heaven and on earth. But we must be clear. Jesus did not begin at Bethlehem, nor did he become the Son of God at his baptism, as some suggest. He was, is and ever shall be God the eternal Son. When we think of him, God's promised Christ, we must learn to think of the pre-incarnate Christ, the incarnate Christ, and the glorified Christ. Some carols reflect this, but they can become so familiar that we miss their glorious meaning.

> Lo! within a manger lies,
> He who built the starry skies.[6]

> He came down to earth from Heaven
> who is God and Lord of all.[7]

This is the Word, the speech, the message of God's salvation, who came to us in a way that we can grasp and understand, yet without fear. But Paul refers to him here as our example.

Humbled for a season

Read also Isaiah 53:1-12

This glorious person, Son of God and King of glory, refused to claim his rights or to enjoy the privileges he was entitled to. Place, power, recognition and reward were his entitlements; but he yielded them all to the Father's will and service. When Paul says, 'He made himself nothing' there is no suggestion that our Lord in any way became less than he was, the eternal Son of God. He did not stop being God when he became truly man. Nor did he become part-God and part-man. Two perfect and distinct natures, the Godhood and the manhood, were perfectly joined together in one person. Consider the words in Wesley's carol:

Veiled in flesh the Godhead see;
Hail! the incarnate deity...
Mild He lays His glory by.[8]

He willingly left the glory of heaven and came down to such a world as this. During his life he again left the presence of the glory of God when he came down to the dark valley of human need from the Mount of Transfiguration (Matt. 17:1-9). He emptied himself of all but love, as Wesley says, and bled for Adam's helpless race. He became a servant. Can any mere illustration make it any clearer? Think of the Queen sweeping the streets, emptying rubbish bins, working in the kitchen in a hostel for the homeless or queuing for a bed for the night. Scripture tells us that the Son of Man had no place of his own to lay his head (Luke 9:57-58). The King was born in a stable. He went about unrecognized, even though his words had a special ring about them (John 7:45-46; Mark 1:21-22). He became God's sin-bearer. He who knew no sin was made sin for us (2 Cor. 5:21).

What a Saviour!

Read also Luke 4:1-15

The eternal Son was born in the likeness of men, in human form. He was not just *like* a man, he was a *real* man. He was tempted in every way, just as we are (Heb. 4:15). He suffered, being tempted (Heb. 2:18). He went through all the stages of growing up through childhood and adolescence to adulthood in the ordinary everyday life of Nazareth. There were no haloes. His circumstances were like ours, for he lived in the real world, in the atmosphere of cruelty, hypocrisy, ruthless government, suspicion, criticism and rejection of his person as well as his ministry.

We need to remember that, in the perfect circumstances and atmosphere of the Garden of Eden, the first Adam was tempted and failed. In the wilderness, with circumstances totally against him and in complete isolation, Jesus, the second (or last) Adam, faced the devil and conquered (Luke 4:1-15). It was as a real man, not as God, that Jesus knew the power of evil and temptation to the fullest extent. *We* have never met the full force of evil because we yield long before it has reached its peak. Hebrews 5:8 records that Jesus learned obedience through the things he suffered; that is, he learned to live the life of faith. In every sense Jesus became one of us and shared all our experiences, but without sin. In that one sense we have to see him as different from us. But there is an important lesson to learn. In the human life of Jesus we are shown that a knowledge, or experience, of sin is not necessary in order to be fully and truly human and to live as God made us to live. It was this perfect Man who died to pay the price of sin, something we could never do for ourselves. Hallelujah, what a Saviour!

The one true sacrifice

Read also 1 Peter 2:21-25; 3:18

The sinless Man made full and perfect atonement for sin when he went in glad but costly obedience to the cross. It was a once-for-all sacrifice for sin as Hebrews 1:1-3; 9:11-14,24-26; and 10:12 make plain. Paul does not *here* expound the meaning of the cross in terms of the doctrine of the atonement because his purpose is to encourage the believers regarding their life and service, rather than to bring outsiders to a knowledge of salvation. We can assume that the message of salvation which had revolutionized lives in Philippi was still being preached. The theme of salvation will be taken up in chapter three. But there is an important lesson here for the church in our own day. We may not and must not preach the *application* of gospel principles to individuals and to society without making sure that the basic message of salvation from sin, justification by faith and reconciliation to God has been made clear. No one can live a Christian life without first becoming a Christian. Sin in its guilt and power has to be dealt with. This is exactly what Jesus came to do and actually accomplished in his death on the cross. Read Romans 8:1-4; 1 Peter 2:24; 3:18; 1 John 2:1-2; and Isaiah 53:4-7,10-12.

There is no doubt that Paul is here speaking of Jesus as the great God-given sin-bearer, who took our sins and paid their price. He substituted for us. He took our place. Think of Barabbas, the convicted man, standing and looking at the cross, and thinking, 'I should have been there.' Let the focus be on Jesus. He emptied himself, he humbled himself. He took the form of a servant. He went to the cross. He laid down his life willingly (John 10:17-18). All that he did, he did for you and me, for our salvation.

To God be the glory

Read also Acts 1:1-11

Although there is no specific mention of the resurrection it is obviously assumed in the declaration of Christ's exaltation to the right hand of the Father. We have considered the pre-incarnate Christ, the incarnate Christ, and now we focus on the glorified Christ. This is all very practical in terms of living the Christian life and engaging in the service of the gospel. The work of salvation is complete and secure. God has declared it to be so. No longer must we think of the Saviour only as despised and rejected by men, a Man of Sorrows. We must see him crowned with glory and honour. Jesus Christ is Lord in every sense of the term. All the issues of redemption history have been secured in his hand (Heb. 9:12). All the persons and powers of heaven and earth and hell must bow, and will bow to him, not just at the end time of history, but now and in every development of human experience.

The victory of the cross is not just a theological proposition, it is a practical fact, being worked out from generation to generation, whether we see it or not, whether we are aware of it or not. This is the basic fact underlying the whole of life: JESUS CHRIST IS LORD. This is what was preached in the first evangelistic sermon at Pentecost (Acts 2:36). This is what Paul expounded at the heart of the doctrine of the resurrection in 1 Corinthians 15:20-28,58, applying the truth to encourage believers to go on in service in the knowledge that it is not in vain. Both here (v. 11) and in Corinthians the final focus is that God's glory should be everything. It is when man insists on being the centre that all the problems begin.

Christ is our life

Read also Ephesians 3:14-21

In verse 9 the word 'therefore' points to God's response to the perfect obedience of his Son in the work of salvation. In verse 12 the same word points to the encouraging call to every believer to work out in life the salvation that is given in Jesus Christ. We must grasp the truth about what Christ has done for us and has given to us, which is now our practical possession by the Holy Spirit who lives within us (Rom. 5:5). The basic pattern of that outworking has already been indicated in verse 5, with the call to have the mind of Christ in us and among us.

We must be quite clear that Paul is not urging us to work *for* our salvation. No sinner is saved by works, only by God's grace (Rom. 3:19-20; Eph. 2:8). But, having been given salvation and salvation-life in Jesus Christ, we must work it out and continue to work it out so that it will be expressed in our personalities, our lives and our service. To do this we need to understand what we have been made and what we have been given in Christ. We are new creatures (2 Cor. 5:17) for whom there is no longer condemnation (Rom. 8:1); for whom all things work together for good (Rom. 8:28); who can depend on God to provide all that is necessary and good for us (Rom. 8:32); and who can never be separated from the love of God (Rom. 8:35-39). Paul is not talking about a way of life far beyond our capacity, because the life of Christ, in all its potential, capacity and blessing is within us by the Holy Spirit who has been given to us. Christ *is* our life, and the life we live is his life in us (Gal. 2:20).

God's provision

Read also Romans 8:5-11

The word translated 'dear friends' is full of deep feeling and indicates the love and affection that must always be in the heart of a true biblical pastor and teacher as he urges his people to go on with Christ into full surrender and service. In Christian life we must work at it with a total commitment as if everything depended on us. But we must also work with a total dependence on God, because it is he who is at work in us, for us and through us by his ever-active indwelling Holy Spirit.

Here Paul is helping us to understand, at least in some measure, God's dealings with us. God is working in us to create the desire to do his will. He is instructing, inspiring and stimulating that desire so that more and more we want to please him. This encourages us to be in earnest about our Christian lives, taking ourselves to task, dealing with our innate laziness and tendency to be disorganized. It takes effort, discipline and determination, not least because we are going against the tide of society and the downward drag of fallen humanity. But we must see that, in and through it all, God is at work, sorting out, developing and balancing our personalities and lives so that we will grow to become our real, redeemed selves. God will see of the travail of his soul and be satisfied, and we shall be immensely grateful for the way he leads us into life in its fulness (John 10:10; Col. 2:9-10). God with us; God in us; God for us. And God has a clear and balanced view of what he plans for us in every area of life and service. He is working to the future and we should anticipate that future, even though it may cause us a little temporary alarm when we consider our limitations. Read Jeremiah 29:11 and 1 Corinthians 2:9.

Be like Jesus

Read also 1 Peter 2:18-23

Working out the salvation we have in Christ means working out the thoughts, attitudes and actions of Jesus in all the different areas and experiences of life. Whoever and whatever we are dealing with, we must have the mind of Christ. We must think as he thought, having patience, being understanding, giving people the human dignity they are entitled to. This has all to do with the heart, our inner attitudes, because, as Jesus said, it is out of the heart that the issues of life come (Matt. 15:16-20).

It is all too easy to blame our circumstances for our personal failings. Secretly, if not openly, we may even blame other people: their actions or failure to act, their attitudes of approval or criticism. But in his earthly life Jesus was constantly among people who chose to misunderstand and who preferred to criticize rather than listen to what he said. Yet Jesus always remained calm. He was always full of grace as well as truth; always aware of the work his Father had given him to do; and careful to make sure nothing hindered or cast a shadow on the work or on the Father's good name. This is the example we have to follow. Consider 1 Peter 2:18-23. Jesus was never 'touchy', never two-faced or deceitful. He was reviled but he did not answer back because he entrusted himself to God who judges justly. His confidence was in the God who works out his good and perfect will in the lives of his trusting people. This does not mean in any sense that Jesus was 'soft'. In the right situations and at the right times he spoke with devastating bluntness, as is seen, for example, in Matthew 23:1-7,13-15. But it is best and safest if *we* put a guard on our tongues and think well before we speak (Ps. 39:1; James 3:3-10).

No grumbling

Read also Exodus 15:22 - 16:3

Paul speaks to individual believers in the context of the life of the congregation. This is wise because if we are not able to behave like Jesus in the company of fellow-Christians, we are not likely to have much witness or influence out in the world where the atmosphere is at least unfriendly and at worst devilish (1 John 5:19). There is something sweeping about the call, 'Do everything'. This includes our normal duties, those extra things we are asked to do with little notice, and the things we are called to do that seem to be far more in number, far more onerous, less public and less praiseworthy than is the lot of others. There must be no grumbling.

Think of the story of Israel in the Old Testament after the Exodus. They were a people redeemed by God, owing everything they had and hoped for to God; but whenever they came under pressure or faced difficulty and self-denial was required, they murmured and complained (Exod. 17:1-3). There are warnings regarding this in 1 Corinthians 10:1-13. We need to examine ourselves.

Some people never really express heartfelt praise to God as the psalmist does (Ps. 103:1-22). Some speak only when there is something they want to criticize or complain about. Paul also forbids arguing or disputing (v. 14). He is referring to the attitude that is always confrontational and delights in causing disagreements between people. Grumbling and arguing are not marks of grace and are certainly not attractive. They are not an expression of the mind of Christ. Do everything without complaining. That is the standard.

Shine as lights

Read also Ephesians 5:1-8,15-20

People living in a crooked, perverse and depraved generation are constantly grumbling and arguing because they
are essentially self-centred. Christians should be different,
otherwise they have no witness and they do not shine as
lights in the midst of spiritual and moral darkness. The
passage in Ephesians 5 shows the standard the early apostles and missionaries expected of their converts. Modern
evangelism has a lot to learn about preaching the gospel.
We need to look for changed lives not just 'decisions for
Christ'.

We are called to be blameless in relation to others and
pure or innocent in ourselves. To be blameless is to live
your life above reproach so that no one can say, 'If he is a
Christian, I want nothing to do with God or the church.'
We are to walk in the light with God (1 John 1:5-7), out in
the open with God, with nothing to hide. We must aim to
live so that we will have a clear conscience (Acts 24:16; 1
Tim. 4:16; Titus 2:6-8). We are also to be innocent, not in
the sense of being easily taken in but, as Jesus said, wise as
serpents and harmless as doves (Matt. 10:16, AV). Paul
speaks of being wise about what is good, and innocent about
what is evil (Rom. 16:19). To be blameless and without fault
is a very high standard but it is an exhortation that is given
again and again (1 Cor. 1:8; Col. 1:22; 1 Thess. 3:13; 5:23).
It is by being different in attitude and practice that Christians shine as lights in society. We all know how dark a
street can seem if even one or two street lamps are out. We
know the problems if the headlights of our cars become
dirty. It happens without our noticing. The same can happen to our lives.

Clean lives

Read also Hebrews 5:11 - 6:3

How do we keep our lives clean so that the light of Christ can shine through us? One answer is in Psalm 119:11 and Paul urges this on the Philippians. They are to hold fast (RSV), hold on to (NIV footnote), or hold out the word of life. The first emphasis has to do with our personal devotional life and the need to *study* as well as to read the Scriptures. We also need the instruction of the Word so that we will be able and competent to give a reason for the faith and hope we have as Christian believers (1 Peter 3:15-16). It is as we read, study, digest and respond to the Word of God that we grow in grace and maturity, our lives becoming ever more stable and dependable. We are to desire and hunger for the pure milk of the Word in order to grow (1 Peter 2:1-3). An appetite for God's Word is a good indication that spiritual life is really there! But we must go on to desire the stronger meat of the Word rather than be content to stay as spiritual babies who need to be carried and coaxed by the church rather than becoming adult workers (Heb. 5:11 - 6:3).

We need to range through *all* the Scriptures, which are given by God to equip us to be his servants (2 Tim. 3:14-17). The phrase 'the word of life' could well refer to Christ himself. It is as we hold fast to Christ that our conversion is confirmed and those who have preached to us see that their labour has not been in vain. If we read the verse as 'holding out' the word of life, then Paul is speaking of witness, proclaiming the gospel by speech and by manner of life. Let your light shine, said Jesus (Matt. 5:14-16). Live a life worthy of the gospel, said Paul (Eph. 4:1). If the lives of Christians stop shining, then the world will become a very dark place.

Keep right on

Read also Acts 20:17-24

In Philippians we see Paul as preacher, teacher and pastor, a man committed to the service of Christ and the gospel. His care for his converts is clear in that he was prepared for his life to be poured out as a sacrifice for the confirmation of their faith. He was basically proud of the Philippians (v. 16) because, in spite of difficulties and limitations, they were persevering. When he wrote to the Thessalonians, who had had a very short time of ministry (Acts 17:1-3,10), he made plain he was indeed proud of them also (1 Thess. 1:2-8; 2:17-20). When John the Apostle was an old man, he expressed his heart by saying that his deepest joy was to see his spiritual children going on in discipleship (3 John 4). In contrast, Paul was deeply concerned about the Galatian believers because they were compromising the truth of the gospel (Gal. 1:6-9; 4:8-11).

Here in verse 17 he speaks again of the real possibility of martyrdom facing him. It is not easy to consider the prospect of having very little time left for both service and life. But Paul speaks of these things as if the fact of his going on resolutely and gladly to the end would be an encouragement to the Philippians to confirm their own commitment to Christ. The drink offering in Jewish ritual was the final small addition that completed the sacrifice. If this was what Paul had in mind, then the real offering being made to God was the faith of the Philippians, and Paul's death, if it came to martyrdom, was simply the 'finishing touch' on another's sacrifice. What humility there was in Paul! He did not regard himself as important. His joy was to be a servant of Christ and Christ's people, and he wanted his friends to have the same joy.

Guidance

Read also Psalm 121

There is something wonderfully human, attractive and encouraging about genuine spirituality. It is a pity that sometimes, perhaps in order to show our spiritual maturity, we give the impression that we are sure about everything, and that we can cope without help. Paul was too honest to be like that. Here he can only say that he *hopes* to send Timothy (v. 19) and that depended on how his own uncertain circumstances worked out (v. 23). He had already expressed his desire to visit Philippi again but almost immediately he had expressed uncertainty over the possibility (1:27). This uncertainty was no doubt caused by the fact that Paul was in prison, but it is doubtful if his decision would be made simply on the basis of personal freedom. Just because something *can* be done, it does not necessarily follow that it *should* be done.

Note the words 'in the Lord' in verses 19 and 24. Paul's attitude to life and service was one of waiting on the Lord and looking to him in faith, not in fear, trusting that he would guide him surely and at the right time. Paul will not presume upon God. He would not make decisions and act on them *hoping* that it would work out. He looked to God for assurance and confirmation, not just for permission. We see examples of this in 1 Corinthians 4:18-19; 16:5-7; 2 Corinthians 1:15-17; and Acts 18:21. Sometimes guidance did not come easily, as in the process of being led to Philippi (Acts 16:6-10). But there is another factor in guidance. In 1 Thessalonians 2:17-18 Paul speaks of being hindered by Satan. Just exactly what that meant we do not know. It reminds us that there is an enemy. But Paul is confident in God and he rests in that.

Young and dependable

Read also 2 Timothy 1:3-9

Paul's gracious humanity is seen in his references to Timothy. The senior man, who had such a driving personality and rich experience, expresses his confidence in the young, sensitive and hesitant man, the son of a mixed marriage (2 Tim. 1:3-5; Acts 16:1-3). Young though Timothy was, Paul recognized in him the marks of true pastoral capacity. He was aware that this young man, who was to have a significant ministry after Paul was dead and gone, could already be trusted with spiritual service. The quality and dependability of Timothy made Paul say he had no one like him. Too many of Paul's colleagues seem to have allowed self-interest to intrude and therefore to hinder and even misdirect their service for Christ and his church.

This is a constant danger. It can arise and become established in various ways. Some may feel they have not been rightly recognized in areas where they feel they have gifts. Some allow personal likes and dislikes and personality clashes to influence their attitudes and actions so that, instead of the work of God being handled in co-operation and fellowship, a spirit of competition intrudes. Behind Paul's words here there is reference back to the 'mind of Christ' and his self-surrender in order to be God's servant. There is a further reference to the quality of Timothy and his service in verse 22, where Paul makes plain just how much Timothy's love and loyalty had meant to him in his costly service. Paul's experience was very like that of our Lord, for he had few who really entered into sharing the costly and often lonely work of ministry. Read the poignant words in 2 Timothy 4:9-17 and Psalm 142:4. Should such loneliness occur? Can it really be avoided if we walk as Jesus walked?

Good and faithful servant

Read also Romans 16:1-7

What a tremendous description we have of Epaphroditus. In Christian terms he was a brother, worker, soldier, messenger and minister, with a heart of care for young converts. He had known serious illness to the point where his friends wondered if he was going to live. He had been sent by the church in Philippi to bring a gift to Paul and to minister to him in whatever way was needed. The quality of fellowship between this man and his home congregation is expressed in verse 26. No doubt their care had been communicated to him, as well as expressed in prayer to God. It was a great relief when his health recovered. Paul did not like the thought of continuing his work without this good man who was indeed a 'gift from God'. And yet he was glad to send Epaphroditus home for the Philippians' sake so that they would have such a man to minister to them.

Perhaps verse 29 shows that Paul was aware just how fickle appreciation and loyalty can be, even among Christians, especially when someone has been absent from their own church for a time. As a missionary prepared to come home, towards the end of a long spell of service, she asked: 'Will the congregation still remember me?'

When there are interesting letters from missionaries telling of successes or crises it is easy to pray. But when, for good reasons, there are few letters, do we forget? Paul reminds the Philippians to honour men such as Epaphroditus and points out something the Christians did not know and the man himself would not mention. He had risked his life to fulfil the task his home congregation had given him. Only in heaven will we see and recognize the scars some men and women carry because of their faithfulness.

Taking stock

Read also Romans 8:31-39

When Paul said 'Finally', it does not mean he was virtually at the end of his letter. His call to rejoice, the last main theme of his letter, is taken up again in 4:4 and some consider the whole section 3:2 - 4:3 to be something of a digression from the main theme. The word 'finally' could be taken to mean 'As I have been saying' and Paul goes on to point out that repetition is often a good thing so that the message is pressed home in a way that people will not forget. The verse could mean, 'In the light of all that I have said, rejoice in the Lord'.

What then have been the main emphases so far in Paul's letter? He has highlighted partnership in the gospel (1:5); confidence in God (1:6); prayer (1:9,19); the overruling providence of God (1:12); the need for a life worthy of the gospel (1:27); the inevitable conflict that faithful service brings (1:29); the example of Jesus (2:5-8); the Lordship of Christ (2:9-10); the life of salvation (2:12-13); and the call to be lights in a dark world (2:15).

In his references to Timothy and Epaphroditus Paul has been pointing to the future and, in relation to all that lies ahead (so much of it quite unknown), he calls the Christians to rejoice in the Lord. It is not a rejoicing that ignores the facts and problems. Faith does not require us to shut our eyes. We face everything in the Lord because we believe truly that he *is* the Lord of all. We rejoice because Christ is preached (1:18). We rejoice even when service is costly (2:17-18). We rejoice because the day of the Lord is at hand (4:4-5), whether it is a day when he shall show his power, or the day when he comes in his glory. We should not weary of this kind of repetition.

Danger exposed

Read also Acts 15:1-11

Paul's rejoicing was realistic. He did not close his eyes to
the situation. He warns of three different kinds of danger,
three aspects of the influence certain people were exercising. We cannot be sure if these people were inside the
congregation or operating from outside. It is clear from Jude
3-4; Acts 20:29-31; and 1 Corinthians 15:12, that quite early
in the life of the church there were those who were accepted members but who had departed from the faith. They
were no longer spiritually motivated and were a danger to
the life of the congregation. Paul speaks plainly although
he does not name names. He describes some people as
'dogs', an offensive term which probably related to the
prowling, scavenging dogs that were common in the streets.
He may be thinking of people who dogged his footsteps,
always snapping and snarling. These are the kind of people
who are always quick to grasp any opportunity to hurt or
hinder what God is manifestly doing. Paul goes on to speak
of evil workers, people who never seem to get tired in their
activities. But what they are doing is not for the good of
God's work. These are people who are always insisting that
something 'extra' or 'special' has to be added to Christian
life to make sure it is truly spiritual. This is a denial of, and
a distraction from, the sufficiency of Christ.

The reference to the mutilation of the flesh is a direct
denunciation of those from an orthodox Jewish background
who insisted that the rite of circumcision, and the allied
submission to the strict letter of Jewish law, were necessary before a person could claim to be a Christian. But if
we add anything to Christ as being necessary for salvation,
then we are denying Christ.

True spirituality

Read also John 4:19-26

It is always a danger when Christian life is allowed to lapse into outward forms or rituals. These do not help us to deny and to deal with the stirrings of the flesh within us. Christ, in whom fulness of life is found, is all we need (Col. 2:6-12). Genuine spirituality is inward, of the heart, and only then can it be expressed in the life and worship that please God. The true people of God, the 'circumcision', those marked out for God, worship God in spirit, that is, by the Holy Spirit. This could refer to the pure and contrite heart spoken of in Psalm 51:6-10,17. It can also be linked with the reference to worship in spirit and in truth in John 4:19-26: not Spirit without truth or truth without Spirit. In like manner truth must always be allied to grace and grace to truth (John 1:14). If sound biblical doctrine is believed and preached in a way that is cold, formal and graceless, there is something very wrong. True worship will always bring mind, heart and will to God's Word, and through that Word to Christ, and through him to the Father, in and by the enabling power of the Holy Spirit.

The second mark of spirituality is that people glory in Christ Jesus. It is when we recognize that Christ is all we need, and that all God has to give to us is in Christ, that we show ourselves to be truly the people of God. Christ is everything. Our attitude must be Christ-exalting, Christ-sufficient, Christ pre-eminent. The delight of the heart of God the Father is great when all attention is on his Son. Think of Paul's words in 1 Corinthians 2:1-5; Colossians 1:15-19; and Ephesians 1:3-8. He certainly glories in Christ Jesus. It is as Christ is glorified that the Spirit is given. That may explain in some measure the dryness of our spiritual service.

Not I, but Christ

Read also Luke 18:9-14

These verses deserve careful study. To be a Christian, to be pleasing to God and to be useful in service require us to have no confidence in the flesh. We may not be as blatant as the man described in Luke 18:9-14, but spiritual self-confidence can arise in a very subtle way. Remember the words of the Spirit to the churches in Ephesus and Laodicea (Rev. 2:1-5; 3:14-17). In the area of Christian service we can easily slip into the attitude that it is by our competence, our capabilities, our spirituality and our prayers that God's work is done. We forget that apart from Christ we can do nothing (John 15:5; 1 Cor. 3:5-7).

It is so easy to become too aware of our background, social standing, education, finance, personality and even our long years of church membership and service, and to assume therefore that we have spiritual significance. But the moment 'self' begins to intrude, the focus and confidence of our lives begin to move away from Christ. Christ is our salvation. Christ is our life (Col. 3:1-4). Christ is our hope. Christ is the one in whom we glory (Gal. 6:14). In the context of Christ's Transfiguration, recorded in Mark 9:2-8, the ultimate focus was not on the experience of the disciples, wonderful privilege as that was, but on Jesus only, and the command to listen to him. Hebrews 12:1-2 has the same emphasis, insisting that we should look away to Jesus. The hymn, 'Just as I am',[9] says it all beautifully.

> Just as I am, poor, wretched, blind,
> Sight, riches, healing of the mind,
> Yea, all I need, in Thee to find,
> O Lamb of God, I come.

Religious or Christian

Read also Romans 9:1-5; 10:1-3

Paul now begins to speak personally, explaining the whole principle and motivation of his life as a Christian. He had a tremendous religious background, and that is something to be grateful for. From childhood he was taught the things of God (Acts 22:3-5) and grew up with a thorough knowledge of the Old Testament, committed to the way of life followed by all earnest Jews. This is a great contrast to the tragic situation in our own generation in which children are growing up virtually in total ignorance of the Bible, often being taught in school that all religions are really saying the same thing. Do we pray about this? Do we pray for Christian teachers? Do we pray for children growing up in a mentally and morally polluted society? In Paul's case his religious and scriptural training did not lead him to Christ and, in fact, bred in him a deep antagonism towards the gospel. Today, in many congregations, the most dogged opposition to the gospel comes from 'church people'. Why should this be?

Romans 9:1-5 states the privileges and blessings of being taught in the things of God, while Romans 10:1-3 shows where the problem arises. Many religious people seek to establish a right relationship with God on the basis of their own efforts. Paul had the mark of God's covenant in circumcision, just as some have the sign of the covenant having been baptized; but that does not make anyone a Christian. Neither does taking Communion, nor service to the church, nor service to the community, nor prayers and studying the Bible. Apart from faith in Christ as Saviour, all these count for nothing in terms of salvation, and may even become a barrier.

Paul's conversion

Read also Acts 9:1-8

Paul's experience on the road to Damascus, recorded in Acts 9:1-8, was shattering. He realized that Jesus Christ, crucified and risen, was the Saviour promised by God right throughout the Old Testament. He discovered that he had been completely wrong about God, Christ and salvation. The very things in his religious life that he had been proud of were the things that had kept him from God. He had come to a crossroads. Would he persist in going his own way, insisting that God should accept him on the basis of all his great efforts and religious commitment, or would he yield and follow God's way of salvation?

God's grace was irresistible; the decision was made, and then it was worked out in the whole of his life in a gloriously radical way. All that he had based his life on up to this point he counted as loss. Of course, he did not lose the *benefit* of all his teaching and training in the Scriptures. That was all kindled in a new way, with new light and new understanding. Note that Paul did not speak about giving up his sins. There is no virtue in that because none of us has any right to our sins. What then did he give up?

He surrendered his self-righteousness and acknowledged that he needed to be saved by God's grace like every other sinner, as he expounds in Romans 3:1-2,9-20. But turning to and following Christ in this radical way cost him his religious acceptability, popularity and prospects. His fellow Jews despised, discredited and persecuted him all through his ministry. His intellectual acceptability was yielded, because the 'wise' of the world despise the message of the cross (1 Cor. 1:18-25). It was costly, but not all cost, for he had Christ.

Knowing Christ

Read also Acts 1:1-11

In verse 8 Paul speaks of how knowing Christ as Saviour and Lord far surpasses any cost involved. He sees himself for time and for eternity 'in Christ'. In 2 Corinthians 12:2 he describes himself as 'a man in Christ'. In Ephesians 2:4-7 he speaks of the believer as being seated with Christ in the heavenly places. In verse 9 of the portion of Scripture we are considering today, he goes on to speak of a right-eousness, or a right standing with God, that has come from God and has been accepted by faith. This is Paul speaking about the salvation he has in Christ. Compare Romans 5:1-2 — emphasizing the three great words, peace, grace and glory — and Romans 8:1,31-39. As we think of this salvation in Christ we do well to think of Wesley's marvellously descriptive words, 'Clothed in righteousness divine'.[10]

Paul was so thrilled and captivated by this great salvation that he wanted to experience it to the full, and he expresses this in terms of knowing Christ. It is something very personal and it has to do with a developing relationship. Paul wanted to know in increasing measure the resurrection power of Jesus Christ operating in his life. He longed that all believers should experience this, as can be seen in his prayer in Ephesians 1:15-20. But Paul was aware that fellowship with Christ is not all blessing and happiness, for it would draw him, and us, into sharing Christ's sufferings in a world that always wants to crucify him. Jesus himself made this plain in John 15:15-21; 16:33. But suffering is not without point or significance and certainly not negative. Paul speaks of sharing in the sufferings of Christ as being for others (2 Cor. 4:7-12).

Sharing his sufferings

Read also 1 Peter 4:12-16

For Paul, the life of the Christian believer is a life of union with Christ in his death and resurrection. The classic expression of this is found in Romans 6:1-14. All the battles and struggles of life and service are engaged in on the basis of the victory Christ won in his death and resurrection, the victory that has been given to us. The active agent in the outworking of that victory in our lives is the Holy Spirit who indwells every believer. That there will be struggles and costs of various kinds Paul makes very clear to the Philippians. In verse 11 he is not expressing doubt about his final salvation but rather affirming that, whatever the cost, he was going to press on in Christ and with Christ, right to the glorious end.

Paul has spoken about becoming like Christ in terms of sharing in his sufferings. He also has in mind the idea of being conformed to the likeness of Christ (Rom. 8:29). This throws light on the meaning of many of the battles that are part and parcel of Christian life. We must not think that 'sufferings' that come in the life of discipleship signify that there is something wrong. It is certainly true that wrong actions, attitudes and reactions to people and situations can cause us turmoil and complications; but even then, we know that in all things God works for good, and for the good of his people. We begin to see that tribulations are God's gracious gifts to help us on to glory. But the benefit of the battles and sufferings operates far beyond the narrow confines of our own little lives. Read Romans 5:3-5; James 1:2-4; and 1 Peter 4:12-16. God is at work in us, for us and through us. That explains the reason for many of life's costly experiences, which we may not fully understand until we get to heaven.

Which world?

Read also 2 Corinthians 5:1-10

Concentrate on verse 11 and Paul's conscious awareness of, and preparation for, the world to come. He lived his whole life aware of the fact that death was not a terminus but the beginning of life and service in an entirely new dimension. He was determined to be ready for that day and for that new service. He speaks of these things in passages such as 2 Corinthians 4:16-18; 2 Timothy 4:6-8; and in a slightly different way in 2 Corinthians 5:1-10. This forward look is expressed clearly in Hebrews 11:8-10 and in 1 John 2:28, where it also contains a challenge to be ready. We need such reminders because it is all too easy to yield to the influence, atmosphere and pressures of society so that we become totally preoccupied with this present world, which will not last. We forget about the world to come and make no preparation for it.

Christians need to ask themselves which world takes priority in their lives. This heavenly perspective is not escapism. It is realism. Paul was sure about that. It is easy to laugh and to say that some people are so heavenly minded they are no earthly use. That can be true! But some are so bound up in this material world that they are of no heavenly use. God works to make us the right kind of people for the real and eternal world. J. B. Phillips translates James 1:2-4 this way: 'When all kinds of trials and temptations crowd into your lives, my brothers, don't resent them as intruders, but welcome them as friends! Realize that they come to test your faith and to produce in you the quality of endurance. But let the process go on until that endurance is fully developed, and you will find you have become men of mature character with the right sort of independence.'[11]

An example

Read also 1 Timothy 1:12-17

True Christian maturity involves a right detachment from the hindrances and sins that can so easily make us drag our feet spiritually (Heb. 12:1-2). Paul speaks of the kind of determination that is necessary for living the life of discipleship and service. No true believer will ever think or feel that he has 'arrived', no matter how long he has been converted, how extensive his service, or how spiritual his peers believe him to be. Paul pressed on to grasp ever more firmly the salvation and the service for which Christ had grasped him (v. 12). It *is* a battle, but not an uncertain one, because the power and principle of sin have been broken for us in the death and resurrection of Jesus Christ.

Paul was very aware that the risen Christ had taken hold of him. He had been told from the start that it was for a clear purpose (Acts 9:15-16; 26:12-19), and he was determined to grasp and fulfil that divine and glorious purpose which he considered to be the greatest privilege of his life (Eph. 3:8; 1 Tim. 1:12-17). Paul was not only saved in Christ he was also mastered by Christ, and such was his sense of gratitude and privilege that his whole being was given over to Christ. This spirit of unqualified service is evident in many of his letters. Paul felt under debt to all to preach the gospel (Rom. 1:14-15). He would feel guilty if claiming his rights kept him from doing so (1 Cor. 9:15-23) and he was willing to become all things to all men to win them for Christ. He was willing to be held in contempt and to be made a 'doormat' if that would bring some to Jesus (1 Cor. 4:11-16). What an example to follow!

On to God's future

Read also Hebrews 11:13-16

What a thrill it is to see in Paul, and in any other believer, this eager determined drive to go on in Christ's service, organizing the whole of life in order to be available to the Saviour. There should be nothing forced or artificial about this because in Christ we are called to God's eternal glory and to that end we have been made partakers of the divine nature (1 Peter 5:10; 2 Peter 1:3-4). It should be natural for us to desire to go on in our Father's will. This is a life that is wonderfully guaranteed as 1 Peter 1:3-9 makes plain, and nothing must be allowed to steal its joy and fulfilment from us. Paul is determined to forget the past, refusing to allow either the successes or the failures to keep him from what God had planned for the future.

In one sense we never forget the past, always looking back to the cross, the place of pardon, peace and hope. Of course, there may be things in the past for which we must try to make amends, both by apologizing for any hurt, neglect and cruelty, and also by cultivating new and better relationships. But some wrongs are so far in the past that we can do nothing about them and in that case we must not allow either guilt or remorse to prevent us from going on with Christ. Forgiveness is real, and sins are put away by God, never to be remembered (Heb. 8:12). The picture of Paul pressing on towards the goal is a marvellous one. The drive and enthusiasm he once showed in persecuting the church had been truly converted and brought under the control of Christ. He was in earnest. Nothing was allowed to get in the way (1 Cor. 9:24-27). Here he is speaking to the 'mature', encouraging them to put aside any childish ways and press on in faith (1 Cor. 13:11).

Safe to follow

Read also 1 Corinthians 4:14-16; 11:1

Paul is writing as a pastor as well as a teacher. He has urged the believers to rejoice in the Lord (3:1), to hold fast to what they have been taught and have followed (3:16). When he referred in 3:15 to people thinking differently he was not suggesting that in matters of basic doctrine people are entitled to their own private opinions. He was really saying, 'Test your opinions against what God has said and he will put you right.'

Paul now counsels Christians to be careful about whom they listen to, and to whose influence they yield. Not all within the Christian fold are as true in life and motive as they should be. Paul is clear about the safest way ahead. He puts forward himself and his colleagues as examples to follow. Later in 4:1 he exhorts the Philippians to stand firm in the truth they have been taught. They are to remember whose ministry brought them to Christ, grounded them in Christ and led them on in Christ; those whose love and pastoral care they had good cause to trust. Paul's words in 1 Corinthians 4:14-16 and 11:1 are very moving, but note that he says, 'as I follow the example of Christ'. There is no place for those who try to dominate other people's Christian lives, exercising a tyranny, so that some are more afraid of disobeying their mentor than they are of grieving God. A true pastor will always strive to make people look to Christ and depend on Christ. It is always safe to ask advice and guidance from such teachers. But we need to be aware of where people are leading us. We should also be asking *ourselves* if we are the kind of dedicated Christians that others can follow and learn from safely.

Dangerous people

Read also Ezekiel 34:1-10

Paul's description in verses 18-19 of some in the congregation who exercised influence on others is solemn indeed. The situation made Paul weep because he saw the spiritual danger these people were in and the damage being done to those who were precious to Christ. He tells the Philippians to consider the lives of these dangerous people to see just how different they were from his own. Of course, it takes genuine humility (or great pride) to testify to the integrity of your own life. But Paul could do that (Acts 20:17-21,33-35; cf. 1 Sam. 12:1-5). All who have the care of God's people are answerable to God (Ezek. 34:1-10). Those who teach are subject to a more searching judgement than others (James 3:1).

Paul charges these 'bad influences' with being essentially worldly in their thinking. Their 'god' is their own desires and inclinations. They boast about a way of life they should be ashamed of. They are enemies of the cross of Christ because they are harming, and leading into danger, men and women for whom Christ has died. The way to deal with such people is to see the influence they exercise and avoid them (Rom. 16:17-18; 2 Tim. 3:1-9; 2 John 7-11). Note the earnestness, the discernment and the care with which Paul sought to guard and shepherd God's flock. His words would be resented by those he spoke against. He would be accused of arrogance by those who regarded themselves as being every bit as spiritual as Paul was. But, we are our brother's keeper, and the good of God's flock is more important than what people think of us. It is to God we all answer.

God in charge

Read also 1 Thessalonians 4:13-18

Over against the worldly attitude that motivates some people and makes their influence dangerous, Paul states certain facts in order to reassure and encourage those who want to both be and do right in relation to God. He reminds the Philippian believers (v. 20) that their citizenship is in heaven. In Christ, we belong to that heavenly kingdom, and we are entitled to its privileges and protection. The Philippians would respond to this because, living in a city that had Roman status, they were well aware of the benefits. All sorts of harmful influences would be restrained by the rule of Roman law, and provisions put in place for the good of the citizens.

So it is with us who are citizens of God's heavenly kingdom. Our lives and needs are under his benevolent government. God takes responsibility for us and our times and all their developments are in his hand and his hand alone. The Lord is king, and he rules in the kingdoms of men (Dan. 4:17). He causes his will to be done on earth in the same perfect way as it is done in heaven. It may not *seem* to be so at many different stages in life's experiences, but we live by faith not by sight, and certainly not by subjective experiences. We live our lives waiting and looking for the coming again of the Saviour King in all the glory of his kingdom. This Saviour, crucified and risen, sits at God's right hand (Heb. 1:2-3); he ever lives to intercede for us (Heb. 7:25; 1 John 2:1); he will come again, recognizable to his people (Acts 1:10-11), and in that day every eye shall see him in his glory (Rev. 1:7). For the believer in this grim world, facing life and death, the coming of the King is a fact that brings joy, hope and assurance (1 Thess. 4:13-18).

Look forward to heaven

Read also Revelation 21:1-5

The last two verses of this passage emphasize that when the glorified Jesus returns in person to establish his kingdom we shall be changed (1 Cor. 15:51-53). He will come as undisputed Lord to bring all things into subjection to himself. We have every reason to look forward. In verse 21 the reference to the return of Christ is in relation to our lowly, human bodies, with all their limitations, being changed so that with new bodies our redeemed personalities will be able to be expressed in a way not possible in this world. We will be set free and enabled to be our true selves in serving God, enjoying him and each other in ways that will never be spoiled. Paul teaches that our new bodies will be related to our present bodies in the way the fully matured grain is related to the unimpressive seed (1 Cor. 15:35-44).

A picture reveals its true qualities when it is put in the right frame. Sometimes people try on a new outfit and then reject it because 'it does nothing' for them. One day we will be 'fitted out' with new bodies that will be the perfect vehicle to express our particular personalities in the light and joy of God's eternal kingdom. 1 John 3:1-3 says we shall be like Jesus, bearing the family likeness of all who are born of God; yet each one is uniquely different. How we long to love the Lord more truly and serve him more worthily! We should be encouraged that that time is coming:

> Then we shall be where we would be,
> Then we shall be what we should be,
> That which is not now, nor could be,
>   Then shall be our own.[12]

Heaven is something to look forward to!

Stand firm

Read also Psalm 46:1-11

If we think more than we do about the sovereign and gracious power of God (3:21) we will learn to stand firm. For example, in Ephesians 1:11 we read of the plan and purpose of God who works all things according to the purpose of his own will. In Ephesians 1:20-22 we read of how God has set the risen Christ far above all and made him head over all in the interest of the church. There is not a sin, temptation, defect, evil power — human or demonic — that is able to stand against him. He is able to save to the uttermost of time and need all who come to him (Heb. 7:25). There is simply no limit to what he can do. We really have no grounds for fear or doubt.

Do we ever ponder the biblical truth in the hymn, 'Be still my soul'?[13] It is true that the waves and winds of experience still know the voice of the one who ruled them here below. The fact that God is our refuge and strength is the basis of the call to be still and to know that he, in his own good time and perfect way, is able to subdue all things (Ps. 46:1-3,10-11). It is when we learn to wait on the Lord, instead of trying to rush ahead in our own wisdom and strength (both of which are very limited), that we discover strength to cope that we did not know we had (Ps. 27:14, AV). This is why Paul counsels the believers to stand firm in the Lord. We are to stand our ground even when it appears that all is giving way. Remember, says Paul, that you are loved, longed for and valued; not just by the human pastor but by the great Shepherd of the sheep himself. And, because that is so, we must recall what Paul taught at the start of the letter: that the God who has begun the good work in us will bring it to perfect completeness in the day of Christ. Read 1 Peter 5:10 and 1 Thessalonians 5:23-24.

Potential for trouble

Read also Romans 12:9-21

It is in the context of glorious spiritual teaching that Paul appeals to two women to stop disagreeing and bringing out the worst in each other. He took the risk of naming names because he was aware that the whole congregation knew about this ongoing disagreement. We do not know what could have caused the situation to reach such a stage that Paul had to intervene in this public way. The issue initially could have been a trifling one, which had grown out of proportion and neither woman would give ground.

This kind of situation is 'a happy hunting ground' for the devil, who will fan the flame of disagreement and try to make people in the congregation take sides, so dividing the fellowship. We are commanded in Scripture to do everything we can to maintain the unity of the fellowship (Eph. 4:3) and, as much as is in our power, to live in peace and harmony with each other (Rom. 12:18). The rights and wrongs of a situation are really secondary. If we feel we are in the right then we are, or should be, able to forgive and to help the one we think is in the wrong. If we suspect we are in the wrong, then we are in the position to confess to the person wronged and so to put things right. The one thing we must not do is to '[nurse our] wrath to keep it warm'.[14] Nor must we engage in a crusade to persuade others that we are the one in the right. If we are hurt, and especially if we are angry, then we must take it to the Lord in prayer and let him be judge and doctor. We are not ignorant of Satan's schemes (2 Cor. 2:11) and we must be on our guard. All of us can think of situations in our own experience when we have taken offence and either got angry or sulked. Note the wisdom of Paul in appealing to *both* women. He was a wise pastor.

Commitment

Read also Ephesians 4:29 - 5:2

Something of the poignancy of Paul's appeal to the two women is seen in his reference to the quality of their Christian service. They had worked side by side with Paul in the defence of the gospel. They had contended for the gospel and now they were fighting with each other. What a waste! What a tragedy! What a success for the devil! Paul speaks also of Clement and other fellow-workers about whom we know nothing except that their names are in God's book of life. They and their quality of service are unknown to us, but not unknown to God.

We also have a reference to another man whose name and service are unknown. But one significant thing is recorded. He was a true or loyal yoke-fellow, bound in common spiritual harness with Paul (cf. Matt. 11:28-30). Without doubt Paul appreciated him. There can be a particular loneliness in the experience of those whose calling is to be 'in the front line' in the service of the gospel. But when someone stands with you, is always there, someone to talk to and who talks to you, someone whose very presence encourages your heart, shares the burden and is sensitive to your feelings, such a person is indeed accurately described as a yoke-fellow. There is a double spiritual harness and the load is shared. At the beginning of the epistle Paul spoke with thanksgiving for partnership in the gospel (1:5). Such partners are indeed a gift from God, and deserve our thanks. Their service can often involve effort, sacrifice and even danger. Think of the risk Jonathan took to encourage David in 1 Samuel 23:14-17. Think of how, in 2 Timothy 1:16-18, Onesiphorus may have searched the prisons in Rome to find and to visit Paul. What a contrast to the two who were arguing!

Rejoice!

Read also Isaiah 43:1-4; 49:15-16

These verses warrant a series of sermons. There is first of all a double summons to rejoice, and that rejoicing must be in the Lord. It does not mean we should pretend to be happy when all is going wrong and we are hurting inside. At times, the right reaction to costly and sad circumstances is to weep, and just as we rejoice with those who rejoice, we should weep with those who weep (Rom. 12:15, AV). This is what partnership and sharing are all about.

Yet whatever our circumstances, we must remind ourselves that we are never victims of these circumstances because our times are in God's hands (Ps. 31:15). Nothing has the power to separate us from God's love (Rom. 8:38-39). God knows what he is doing with us, why he is doing it in a certain way, and he walks with us every step of that way (Job 23:10; Isa. 43:1-4). We are to find our joy in the Lord: in who he is and what he has done. He is King of Kings, Lord of Lords, Shepherd, Saviour, Friend, the one who has loved us with an everlasting love (Jer. 31:3). He has secured for us eternal redemption, forgiven all our sins, reconciled us to God, opened the Kingdom of Heaven for us, and given us his great and precious promises, on which we stand and by which we live (2 Peter 1:3-4). Jesus himself has said that no one can pluck us from his hand (John 10:28); that he will never leave us as orphans (John 14:18); and he has prayed that the Father will keep us and bring us to where he is so that we may share his glory (John 17:24). As Christians, we have every right to be confident in our dealing with all the changing circumstances of life. Because we are in God's good hand we do not react in rebellion or self-pity. The facts demand that we should rejoice.

Tell God

Read also Matthew 6:25-34

To have no anxiety about anything seems extreme and indeed impossible for ordinary mortals such as we are. But we are not ordinary, nor do we have to live by our own resources. We have Jesus, and in him all we need is promised and provided. Besides, what does anxiety accomplish apart from making us tired, tense, fretful and difficult to live with? Paul is not asking us to suppress natural feelings of concern but he is insisting that we do not allow a spirit of anxiety to dominate and direct our lives, because that would be a contradiction of faith, suggesting that the Lord may fail to keep us. Think of Jesus' wonderfully calm words in Matthew 6:25-34 and his reassurance in John 14:1-2,25-27. The cure for anxiety is simply to take everything to God in prayer, echoed in the hymn by Joseph M. Scriven:

> O what peace we often forfeit,
> O what needless pain we bear,
> All because we do not carry
> Everything to God in prayer![15]

We are told to cast all our cares and anxieties on God, because he cares about us (Ps. 55:22; 1 Peter 5:7). Sometimes there are things about which people may be so burdened, worried and ashamed that they cannot share them with anyone. They can tell God. He knows. He understands and he cares. We should go boldly to the throne of grace (Heb. 4:15-16). The Holy Spirit can take the ache of our heart and present it as a perfect petition to God (Rom. 8:26). A Christian who had many struggles because of severe war wounds said to his minister, 'When you take your burdens to the cross you should not take them home again.'

Prayer is simple

Read also Luke 11:1-10

Prayer should be the natural reaction of a Christian in all sorts of circumstances. The word 'petition' refers to specific requests when we cry humbly to God for an answer to needs we are feeling deeply and possibly do not understand. But there must also be thanksgiving for answers to prayers and past blessings. Do we thank God for answers as often as we make requests? If we were more grateful to him for all his great faithfulness and his many mercies (Lam. 3:22-23) we would find prayer a more natural ongoing part of our Christian lives. Many find prayer difficult and an illustration from the book *Prayer* by O. Hallesby should help. He tells of how his little son came into his study. The boy knew that he was not supposed to disturb his father when he was working and his conscience troubled him a little. But he said, 'Daddy, I will sit still all the time if you will only let me be here with you.' He received immediate permission. Hallesby says that that is how we often feel with regard to our heavenly Father. We love to be with him, just to be in his presence. Moreover, we never disturb him, no matter when, or how often, we come.[16]

This is a lovely picture of going to God with our prayers. We speak to him about all that concerns us and we know he is glad we have come. That book on prayer begins by referring to Revelation 3:20 and then makes the statement that prayer means that we let Jesus come into our hearts. It is not our prayer that moves the Lord Jesus. It is Jesus who moves us to pray, and in prayer we hand over all the issues that concern us for him to deal with. 'Prayer is the soul's sincere desire, uttered or unexpressed... Prayer is the simplest form of speech that infant lips can try.'[17] Lord, teach us to pray.

God's peace

Read also Psalm 23:1-6

Paul speaks of prayer and peace together. Often in our earnestness we create in ourselves, and sometimes in the fellowship, a spirit of tension and anxiety in the realm of prayer. This should not be, because the God to whom we pray knows what we need before we ask (Matt. 6:8). He is absolutely clear as to his will for the situation we are praying about and equally able to bring it to pass. It is when our minds and hearts are fixed on God that we begin to know his peace. It is not a peace that depends on circumstances nor on our seeing the answer to our prayers. It is supernatural peace; a peace that passes understanding.

Think of the peace and poise that marked the life of our Lord Jesus Christ. He told his disciples that their hearts must not be troubled because he was giving them his peace (John 14:1,27). We do not experience this peace by running away from situations, closing our eyes to problems, or suppressing our emotions. It is the kind of peace spoken of in Psalm 23 as a table of enjoyable rest and refreshing in the presence of the enemy, knowing that between ourselves and the enemy stands God himself. In verse 9 Paul will speak of the God of peace, and Hebrews 13:20 tells us that it is the God of peace who worked the mighty work of resurrection so silently and effectively. It is the God of peace who stands guard over us, bringing his peace to both mind and heart. The subject of peace is glorious and practical. Consider Colossians 3:15: 'Let the peace of Christ rule in your hearts.' The picture is that of a chairman calling a meeting to order. Paul may have been looking at the jailer standing guard over him, allowing no unauthorized visitors. The peace of God was standing guard over Paul's mind and heart in the same way.

Why be anxious?

Read also Isaiah 40:10-11,25-31

Peace of mind and heart is a liberating and empowering blessing, and in God's peace we are able to get on with his work without being unduly distracted. It is the assurance of God's presence, power, purpose and activity that brings peace. In that peace we take charge of our thinking and simply refuse to allow ourselves to rush ahead into all sorts of speculations and possibilities. If we do that, we are simply forgetting about God and believing that everything depends on us. We must not think that we are in charge of everything. Our commitment to biblical doctrine forbids it. We need to centre our thoughts on God and then we can begin to prove the truth of Isaiah 26:3-4.

First of all there is the affirmation that God will keep in peace those whose minds are steadfast, or fixed on him. Then there is the summons to trust, that is, to believe what God has said. This means that we need to be always learning and re-learning what God is like. That requires us to consider closely such passages as Isaiah 40:10-11,25-31. When panic replaces peace we need to ask ourselves if we have forgotten God, or if God has forgotten us. We need to ponder, or, even better, to sing in the metrical version, Psalm 43:3-5. Why are we cast down? Why are we discouraged? Has God retired? Has God opted out of the human situation, leaving it to men and devils to control? The God of peace deals with Satan in no uncertain terms (Rom. 16:20). The God of peace in person is faithful and will keep you (1 Thess. 5:23-24). The peace of God is a wonderful blessing, and when people say they do not know this peace it may be because they never stop their own activities long enough to be aware of it. Do not forget that it was when God allowed Paul to be put in prison that he wrote about this peace.

The peace of Christ

Read also John 20:19-31

It is when we are rejoicing in God that there is a curb on
our anxiety and we can rejoice even in tribulation or
sufferings, as Romans 5:3-5 makes plain. When anxiety is
brought into the presence of the Lord, we become calm
enough to pray rationally, and to pray in faith rather than
in fear. When we take our earnest requests to God in prayer
and begin to be aware that God is indeed involved with us
in every aspect of our lives, peace begins to assert itself.
Life then begins to be more positive, not least because we
are content that God should answer our prayers and deal
with us, and those for whom we pray, in his own good way
and in his perfect timing. Remember that Jesus promised
his disciples his peace when he was about to face the treach-
ery of Judas and the agony of the cross. When Jesus died he
made peace by the blood of the cross (Col. 1:19-20). That
means we can know the peace and calm of sins forgiven.

There is a particular peace that grows and deepens as
we truly commit ourselves to the fellowship of God's people,
and realize that we are never really on our own. In Christ
we become at peace in and with ourselves, accepting that
we are valid and valuable, regardless of our limitations and
complications. Because we have the peace of God in Jesus
Christ we are more able to make room for others, accepting
them and making them feel welcome. Individually and in
fellowship we realize more and more that he is our peace.

Peace, perfect peace, by thronging duties pressed?
To do the will of Jesus, this is rest.[18]

Remember that one of the significant words Jesus spoke to
his disciples immediately after the resurrection was 'Peace'.

Ordering our lives

Read also 2 Timothy 2:14-19

Paul now emphasizes the need to use our minds. This does not mean an occasional spiritual thought in church on a Sunday, but a rigorous ongoing thinking through of the practical implications of what we have been taught. Our experience of the peace of God and our assurance as to the presence of the God of peace (v. 9) is not something that just happens. It has to be worked at and it has a great deal to do with our thinking. Our thoughts must control and direct our emotions, not the other way round! If emotions are dominant then our handling of life will be largely in terms of reacting to people and to circumstances rather than on the basis of faith. Our thoughts are fed, led, kindled and maintained by what we hear, read, see and talk about. That means we are in the realm of the practical ordering of our lives. We are to think about what is true rather than what is false or merely speculative, remembering that Jesus is the truth (John 14:6). Our focus should be on what is noble, worthy of honour and respect, rather than empty and frivolous. We can still laugh because there is humour that is pure and has no need for the sordid and suggestive.

The word 'lovely' should not be understood simply in terms of being attractive, because some people and things that are very attractive are far from being good for us. The word 'admirable' is variously translated 'gracious' or 'of good report' and may refer to things that even pagan society would regard as having real worth. Consider how, in our Lord Jesus Christ, grace and truth were wonderfully brought together. Anything that rightly deserves the name of excellence or virtue, anything that is worthy of both human and God's praise, anything that we would talk about with our family; these are the things we should be thinking about.

Battle for the mind

Read also Romans 1:18-23,28-32

There is a battle going on for the control of people's minds, seeking the eradication of all Christian and moral truths and influences, and the introduction and cultivation of a lifestyle in which there are no objective or absolute standards. This is why, as Christians, we must refuse to let our thinking be squeezed into the mould of this wicked a-moral world (Rom. 12:1-2). It is all too easy to slip gradually into a mindset that simply excludes God. As human nature is fallen and disordered, this in turn leads to a progressive degeneration of behaviour (Rom. 1:28-32). But the problem is even more serious because, as Romans 8:6-8 makes clear, the fleshly, sinful or worldly mind is hostile towards God.

In 1 Peter 1:13 we are urged to prepare our minds for action, and this echoes Paul's exhortation here. In 2 Corinthians 10:5 he speaks about bringing every thought into captivity to Christ. Thoughts lead to imaginations and then to actions. Paul is not teaching here a narrow attitude that would cut us off from the whole cultural life of society, insisting that we read only Christian books and that the only permissible music is that of hymn tunes. That there is danger in some areas of literature and some types of music and lyrics is beyond doubt. But Paul uses the word 'whatever' and indicates a whole range of possible interests, refusing to squash us all into a uniform asceticism. There are misguided Christians who seem to take the attitude that 'If you enjoy it, it must be wrong.' We are told in 1 Timothy 6:17 that God has given us all things in rich measure to enjoy. This is the God who at first set man and woman in the glory of the Garden of Eden. But we must guard against the temptation to transgress and so to spoil it all.

The standard for all

Read also Matthew 23:1-7

There is an important lesson in verse 9 for all who teach others in the things of God. Paul makes it clear that what he has been teaching the believers with regard to faith and life were the things by which he himself lived. That is why he was not afraid to call them to follow his example. He had already made plain in 3:12-14 that he was not in any sense claiming that he had 'arrived' spiritually. But he had drunk deeply at the wells of salvation in Christ, and having learned confidence in God and tasted of his peace, he was a good example to follow. He calls the believers to walk with him along the road marked out by Christ, and there is no doubt that the company of a godly and gracious friend or partner is both an encouragement and a sanctifying influence. Certain friends and acquaintances have the effect of quenching our desire to go with Jesus in true discipleship. Joining with some people in their activities has led us into temptations that we have not always been able to resist. Even when we have resisted, we have been left with a reluctance to 'take up the cross' and follow Christ.

Paul was a true pastor and teacher, and he knew the importance of showing that the sermons he preached to others were first preached to himself. He never set a standard of Christian behaviour that he was not prepared *first* to set for himself. The words 'heard' and 'seen' make clear that Paul practised what he preached. Jesus had devastating words about teachers who could not say that (Matt. 23:1-7), and equally searching words of rebuke for people whose lives did not match their spiritual profession (Matt. 7:15-27). When we are right with God and ordering our lives to please him, we will know his peace.

Financial support

Read also 1 Corinthians 9:3-18

Paul was very human. He needed the kindness and support of the Philippians and he expresses his gratitude to them. He knew they prayed for him and his ministry (1:19). He knew they were glad to be his partners in service (1:5). But spiritual care has to be expressed in human terms, some-times by speech and sometimes by practical help. Paul had previously received monetary gifts from the Philippians for his support (4:16); but more recently, he had been puzzled and perhaps hurt because they seemed to have forgotten his practical needs. Some missionaries we pray for may feel like this when, because of lack of home support, their maintenance allowances cannot be sent to them. A direct gift at such a time can be an incalculable encouragement.

Paul was not too proud to accept such gifts even though he mostly tried to be self-supporting so that no one could slander his motives for being 'in the ministry' (1 Cor. 9:8-18). He defended the principle of 'the maintenance of the ministry' but, when the situation demanded, he supported himself. Paul was always very careful about 'church money' (2 Cor. 8:16-22), appointing others to handle it lest there be any suspicion of corruption. The real point of verse 10 is that spiritual care and partnership were actually expressed in practical human terms. Paul's affirmation that he was neither complaining (v. 11) nor seeking gifts (v. 17) suggests that he was sensitive about being dependent on the gener-osity of other people in his life as a missionary teacher. In Acts 20:33-35 he testified that he earned his own living and paid the expenses of his colleagues so that there would be no distraction from the gospel. Of course, there can be a wrong kind of independence which is really pride, and that has to be guarded against.

Contentment

Read also Hebrews 13:5-8

We have considered Paul as the great teacher whose life exemplified and confirmed his ministry. We saw him earlier as a man confident in God (1:6), earnest and dedicated in his resolute service (3:7-8,12-13). Here we see him content in God (4:11). At the same time, to be supported in God's work by the sacrificial giving of people who may be far from rich is a deeply moving experience, and Paul was not slow to express his thanks to them also. But even in this situation he sought to encourage others by his own testimony. In a whole variety of situations and experiences he had learned to be content. He acknowledges that this did not come easily. He had *learned* progressively that God's will is good, perfect and totally acceptable (Rom. 12:2, AV).

Paul had developed this attitude to life because he had learned the kind of God he had. It was the God of sure guidance who led him to Philippi. It was the God of wise providence who landed him in prison there to further the gospel. It was God who gave his Son to be his Saviour and who gave him good and faithful colleagues to work with. It was God who heard his prayers, caused him to rejoice, and gave him peace that passed understanding. It was the God of all grace who gave him the privilege of preaching the gospel (Eph. 3:8) and who had called him to his eternal glory (1 Peter 5:10). With a faithful, gracious God like that ordering his life, why should he be anything other than contented? Practical human kindness, care and encouragement are still necessary. Just to pray can be the easy way out. It does not disturb our routine. Read Acts 28:14-15 and see the effort some made to encourage Paul after his costly journey. But whatever people did or failed to do, Paul was content.

God knows best

Read also 1 Timothy 6:6-12,17

Paul's spirit of contentment was grounded in the fact that his life was hidden with Christ in God (Col. 3:3). It was because he knew he was in Christ's hand, for life and for service, that he was able to keep going, no matter what happened. He did not cope in some superhuman way but he went through the whole range of ordinary human reactions. 2 Corinthians 2:12-13 shows how he experienced the turmoil of anxiety, worrying about a certain group of Christians to such an extent that he was unable to seize the opportunity to preach. Some who read these words may be a similar distraction to their own minister!

In 2 Corinthians 7:5-7 we see the turmoil in his feelings after having had to exercise discipline in respect of some Christians whose behaviour had been bringing the gospel into disrepute (1 Cor. 5:1-5). In 2 Corinthians 12:7-10 he testified that the costliness of service had led him to plead with God for relief. He felt that if the 'thorn in the flesh' (whether some physical or psychological ailment, or a person who tormented him) was removed, then his service for God would be richer and fuller. But when the Lord made it plain that it was in and through the ongoing painful struggle that he was able to use him in service, then Paul gladly accepted God's ordering of his circumstances. Remember that it is only when our eyes are fixed on Christ that we are enabled to cope with being abased and humiliated, and are also able to keep humble and remain useful when everything is flowing in our favour. Success can be as hard to cope with safely as affliction. Read also the balanced prayer in Proverbs 30:7-9. Paul would have said his 'Amen' to that prayer, and also to the words in Job 13:15 and 23:10.

Caring and sharing

Read also Mark 14:1-9

It is wonderful to see how often and how genuinely Paul expressed his appreciation of all that people did for him. He began to do this in verse 10, and he resumes the theme in verse 14, where we must link the words 'good' and 'troubles'. The tokens of their care and concern had reached him and had encouraged him in his costly work in the gospel. Their understanding support ministered to him just as the actions of the woman in Mark 14:1-9 ministered to Jesus when he was so conscious of his coming agony. A kind act or word, done naturally, can often encourage someone to cope with a spiritual battle.

Another example of this 'sharing' is found in 2 Timothy 1:15-18. Imagine how this visit would have lifted Paul's spirit. Onesiphorus did not say, 'I would have visited but I did not know your address.' He made it his business to find the address. We do not know how far he had travelled, nor how much it cost him in time and trouble. Perhaps he had missed out on some celebration in order to do this kindness to the apostle, to whom he felt a debt of gratitude for spiritual blessings. Paul's relationship with the Christians in Philippi was one of long-lasting fellowship and partnership in which there was great trust. He had shared with them the costly loneliness that he had known over a long spell of service (v. 15), and that is something many are unwilling to do. Of course, to confess your feelings of loneliness can make you vulnerable, because people may respond by pitying, criticizing, despising, or even ignoring you. Paul was glad and grateful that some shared his load and so fulfilled the law of Christ (Gal. 6:2).

Kindness

Read also 2 Corinthians 8:1-7

Friends who go on sharing with us in service and bearing with us in spite of our many complications and failures are a blessing. Paul refers to practical gifts in verses 16-17 but immediately guards himself against the slanders levelled at him by those who said he was too interested in obtaining money. Paul had to do this again and again, as 2 Corinthians 11:7-10 and 1 Thessalonians 2:3-6 demonstrate. In verse 17 Paul rejoices because the Philippians' giving had been a pleasure to God and brought honour to his name. God does indeed love the cheerful giver (2 Cor. 9:7), and values especially those for whom there is a real element of sacrifice in the giving. Remember the widow in Mark 12:41-44 and the principle stated by David in 2 Samuel 24:24. Paul was sure that God would bless the Philippians for what they had done. They would not be the losers, because they would have had a creative share in God's own work for the salvation of others. This was their reward.

The passage in 2 Corinthians 8:1-7 may well refer to the Christian liberality shown by the Philippians, and Paul describes practical giving as a work of grace. He tells them (v. 18) just how amply his heart and life had been filled because of their kindness. Their gifts were like a fragrant offering to God, which had pleased God, and had brought a freshness and blessing to his own life and work. Some of the simplest things we do for love of the Lord prove to be immensely significant. A 'cup of cold water' or a visit can have a rich spiritual value (Matt. 10:40-42). There are many applications of the words 'Touched by a loving hand, wakened by kindness.'[19] That is an element in evangelism that is often forgotten.

Riches in Christ

Read also Jeremiah 1:4-10

As a good pastor, Paul is teaching *and* encouraging his people. He tells them that the God who had ministered to him all through his life and service would do the very same for them. Increasingly as his life went on, Paul was aware of how richly he had been blessed and privileged in the service of the Son of God. Now, recognizing that he might not have much longer to live, all the cost of battle and struggle fades into the background. He was aware of how God's goodness and mercy had followed him all the days of his life, watching over him, guiding and controlling him, just like two well-trained sheepdogs totally obedient to their Master. Paul urges the Philippians to trust this God whose love is everlasting (Jer. 31:3), whose faithfulness is great, and whose mercies are renewed daily (Lam. 3:22-24).

When Paul assures them that God will meet all their needs, he may be contrasting needs with desires, recognizing that sometimes we pray for things that would not be good for us, or may limit our service. But more, he is indicating just how personally and particularly God knows us and deals with us. Read Jeremiah 29:11 and 1 Corinthians 2:9. It is best that we do not know too far in advance what God is planning to do with us in our lives. The sheer dimension of it might either make us insufferably proud (as in the story of Joseph in Gen. 37:5-11), or cause us to be so apprehensive that we draw back in unbelief, as it did with Jeremiah (Jer. 1:4-10) and Moses (Exod. 4:10-13). Try to grasp the amazing scale of God's provision. It is according to his riches in glory in Christ Jesus. If we have Jesus, we have riches beyond calculation, because all the fulness of God is in him (Col. 1:19; 2:9-10) and he lives in us. That is indeed comfort, encouragement and assurance.

A doxology

Read also 1 Chronicles 29:10-14,18,20

It is little wonder that Paul expresses himself in a doxology of praise and worship. We also should review our own lives and consider the love, patience and forgiveness of our God. We need to recognize the changes worked in our lives in the liberation and integration of our personalities. We acknowledge that all that has been accomplished in years of service was indeed the work of the grace of God from beginning to end. Then we say and sing from the heart, 'To God be the glory!'

When we consider the person and the attributes of our God; when we ponder his wise, sure and sovereign providence; and when we really marvel that God spared not even his own Son but gave him up for us all, then we begin to sing in a true spirit of worship, 'How great Thou art!' When we read the great passages of praise and worship such as Romans 11:33-36, we begin to see just how self-centred we are apt to be, almost as if our attitude is that God's chief function is to bless and glorify us. Think of the *Shorter Catechism*'s affirmation that 'The chief end of man is to glorify God and to enjoy him for ever.' Without doubt, it is when we live to please and glorify God that we begin to enjoy him, his company, his service and his people. How easily and superficially at times we say the traditional words at the end of the Lord's Prayer: '*Thine* is the kingdom, and the power, and the glory, for ever.' Read 1 Chronicles 29:10-14,18,20, and then 2 Chronicles 7:1-3 to see how an awareness of God's glory caused the people to give thanks for his steadfast love. Read also Revelation 5:11-14 and 7:9-12 and consider the praises of heaven. Never forget that this great and glorious God is our loving heavenly Father.

A final greeting

Read also Ephesians 2:11-13,19-22

Focusing on the glory of God, Paul is still able to refer to every single saint in Christ Jesus. We do not get lost in the vast concourse of people around the throne of God. The opposite is true. We are found, and we are increasingly made our true individual selves. Think of the reaction of a new convert in Philippi as Paul's words were read to the congregation. The Holy Spirit would assure that person, however lowly and limited, that he or she belonged rightly to the family of God's people. We must never assume that new converts or new arrivals in the fellowship are less valuable than those who have been around a long time. All that we are and have and will ever be is the result of God's grace. There is no place for pride (1 Cor. 4:7).

Paul associates his companions with him in his greeting. All the Christians, including those in Caesar's household, join in the salutation. Yes, there were converts in the most unexpected places; among the military, the civil service, the political executives and among the lowliest slaves in Caesar's household. That is a reminder not to limit God's grace in its working, and not to jump to conclusions that people are not Christians simply because they do not conform to accepted evangelical patterns or do not speak the usual evangelical language. God's Spirit is sovereignly free and he works where he chooses and in whatever manner is right for the situation. Paul's final word focuses on the grace of the Lord Jesus Christ: his free, undeserved, unlimited, never-ending favour and blessing and enabling power. Of course, the grace is never separate from the person, and we are left in the presence of the Son of God, who loved us and gave himself for us. That is the best place to be.

Paul's letter
to the
Colossians

Introduction

Paul begins his letter by affirming his call by God to be an apostle and confirming his belief in the sovereign and perfect will of God. Although he is in prison in Rome, under 'house arrest' with some degree of freedom of activity (Acts 28:16,30-31), he refuses to think that circumstances have cancelled his call to be a messenger of the gospel. Nor does he think that somehow the will of God had been countermanded or limited by the actions of the religious and political powers that had led to his imprisonment. Prevented from continuing his much travelled ministry he used his imprisonment in Rome to write his letters under the inspiration of the Holy Spirit. The group described as his captivity letters includes Philippians, Colossians, Ephesians and Philemon. His last letter, 2 Timothy, was also written from prison in Rome, at a time when he was expecting to die.

When we read the story of the early apostolic church we learn that Paul suffered other unjust imprisonments in Caesarea and Ephesus as well as in Rome. Some suggest Philippians was written from one of these earlier prisons. In the providence of God these experiences, which at first seemed negative and sometimes were very painful, were in fact opportunities to write letters. These were to be great sources of instruction and inspiration for the church for the whole of history. Paul knew the truth of what he wrote in Romans 8:28, that in all things God works for good. However little evidence there may be at the time, the things that happen do in fact work out for the furtherance of the gospel (Phil. 1:12-14). At a first reading some of the verses of Colossians may seem to be very difficult to understand, but remember that this epistle was written by the inspiration of the Holy Spirit to be a blessing to a church of recent converts who were in danger from false teachers. It was not thought too difficult for them.

The city and the letter

Read also Revelation 2:12-17

This letter was written by Paul to a church he had had no part in founding and which he had not visited (2:1). It was delivered by Tychicus and Onesimus (4:7-9) who also carried the letter to the Ephesians and the short letter to Philemon. Colosse was one of three cities about one hundred miles east of Ephesus in Asia Minor. The other two were Laodicea and Hierapolis and by comparison Colosse was small. The whole area appears to have been evangelized by missionaries who had gone out from Ephesus during Paul's two-year stay there (Acts 19:10).

It seems from Colossians 1:7 and 4:12-13 that Epaphras, himself a Colossian, was the evangelist who brought the message of Christ to the city. What a thrill to take the gospel to your own people and to see them coming to faith. But it could not have been easy to preach in these cities. Hierapolis was the 'city of the sanctuary', a centre of pagan cults. Laodicea was rich and self-confident (Rev. 3:14-22). Perhaps the main influence in the wider area was Pergamum, a city under much satanic influence (Rev. 2:12-13). That there was a church at all in Colosse was a miracle of grace and it should encourage all those who feel that they themselves are in a grim and unpromising situation. Epaphras had brought news to Paul about the congregation in Colosse (1:4-8), which prompted this letter, written to meet and to correct specific needs. But the thrust of the letter is more than just correction. The overall theme is the pre-eminence of Christ (1:18). Its aim is 'to show all parts of our salvation are placed in Christ alone'.[1]

The greeting

Read also Matthew 5:13-16

If the believers in Colosse felt themselves very much a minority in the city, and insignificant compared to other churches, Paul's opening words must have thrilled their hearts. He refers to them as holy and faithful brothers. They were holy or saints because God had called them in Christ through the gospel and they were marked out and set apart as God's believing people. They had been 'engraced' individually and corporately. They were God's people (1 Peter 2:9) in that city, called to live for him, not in some isolated monastic kind of situation but right there in the middle of so much that was contrary to God and ignorant of him. They were there to be the salt of society restraining the advance of corruption (Matt. 5:13). They were in place to be the light of the world to shine in the midst of very real moral and spiritual darkness (Matt. 5:14-16; Phil. 2:15). They were set apart for God, but must not try to cut themselves off from any contact with those who were in great need of Christian influence. They had to be like Jesus: separate from sinners (Heb. 7:26), and yet a friend of sinners (Luke 15:1-2).

There is something wrong if Christians have no real friends among unbelievers. This calls for balance and wisdom. In 1 Corinthians 5:9-11 Paul spoke about the need to be among sinners and yet not to be involved with them. John likewise warns about the danger of loving the world (1 John 2:15-17). Of course, to be an effective influence for the gospel both the Colossians and we, ourselves, must understand clearly who we are, what we believe and what we have in Christ. That will be expounded right through this epistle.

The blessing

Read also Numbers 6:22-27

The whole of this epistle is full of detailed teaching about the salvation we have in Christ, and the blessing and power of that salvation in relation to living for Christ in a generation of godless and idolatrous materialism. Paul's objective is clear right from the start. He teaches the truth in order to encourage the believers, and in this greeting (v. 2) he directs both minds and hearts to God from whom all blessing flows. It is important to grasp the truth of Paul's words, which we so often simply pass over in a casual way. Paul does not just *hope* that God's grace will be with us. He assures us that God's spontaneous, freely given, all-sufficient loving kindness, favour and enabling will be with us. When we sing about 'Amazing grace' do we really marvel at it and thrill to the thought that the grace that has brought us safely thus far through life will in fact continue to lead, guide and enable right to the end?

God's peace will also be with us, bringing with it the assurance that we are in his hand and always in his presence. The two words 'grace' and 'peace' speak of the Father's pleasure in his children. There are echoes here of the great Aaronic blessing in Numbers 6:22-27 and also of the words of John 14:27, which speak of a peace the world can neither give nor take away. We need to believe the words of Jesus when he said so clearly, 'My peace I give you.' No one has the right to take from us the assurance which that gift carries. Paul will take up this theme in a practical way when he says, 'Let the peace of Christ rule in your hearts' (3:15). The Colossians, with their restlessness and confusion, needed these words, and so do we. 'Take from our souls the strain and stress, and let our ordered lives confess the beauty of Thy peace'.[2]

Prayer and thanksgiving

Read also 2 Thessalonians 3:1-4

The first lesson here is the vital part thanksgiving plays in prayer, even when praying for people not personally known to us, and especially when praying for those near and dear to us and those with whom we work and worship week by week. Thanksgiving speaks of an attitude that focuses on what is good and commendable rather than on faults, failures and disappointments. Paul could give thanks for the Colossians because they were God's people and therefore precious to him. If God has called people to himself in Christ, paying the price of their redemption, who are we to devalue or denigrate them? Paul's thanksgiving is in part rejoicing that the gospel had reached them. He was thrilled that God had a 'presence' in the city through them. Perhaps he was also thrilled that the outreach from his own ministry in Ephesus, through those converted there and sent out to witness, had a part in this ongoing drama of salvation. If there is joy in heaven over one sinner coming to salvation (Luke 15:7,10) how we should rejoice and give thanks to God for every advance of the gospel, even though the results of ministry may not be visible in 'our place'.

The second lesson we can learn is found in the fact that the great preacher puts such a strong emphasis on prayer as part of the process of establishing and building the church in the world. Prayer is an ongoing ministry, as verse 9 will make plain. It is also a vital factor in the preaching of the gospel, as 4:2-4 will emphasize. It is interesting to note this early emphasis on prayer, especially in view of the tendency of the Colossians to be drawn away to 'higher' spirituality. People who are unduly preoccupied with their own spirituality are seldom people who can be depended on to be intercessors for the Lord's work.

Faith, hope and love

Read also 1 Corinthians 13

Faith is more than just intellectual grasp of and consent to the facts of the gospel. Faith looks to Christ as the only hope of salvation; it commits itself in discipleship; and draws upon the life and power that are in Christ. By faith we are in Christ and Christ is in us. The first and continuing expression of that Christ-life in us is that we will love those who are in Christ. This is the beginning of true Christian fellowship. It will also have the effect of making us desire to draw others in to share this life and fellowship. It cannot be otherwise, for the life in us is the life of the Jesus who came into the world to seek and to save the lost. Love is real and practical, not sentimental and superficial. 1 Corinthians 13 shows us what love is and does. John 15:11-12 and 1 John 4:11 tell us how the *duty* of love is laid on us. It means we *act* lovingly without necessarily waiting for the feelings of love. We do not wait for people to deserve our love. We love because he first loved us (1 John 4:19).

Paul links love with hope, revealing it as the inspiration and power behind both faith and love. If there is no sure hope in the gospel everything remains uncertain. We are saved in hope (Rom. 8:24) and that means that while there is certainty in salvation there is always a 'not yet' element in our experience. It is as our eyes and hearts are set on the sure hope of heaven, the sure hope of victory and the sure hope of Christ's coming again, that both faith and love are kept strong and fresh. Is it not strange how easily we forget about heaven? It is almost as if even Christians think of it as second best rather than a perfect fulfilment. Never be ashamed to speak of the other-worldly element of the gospel. If we have hope only in this life we are to be pitied (1 Cor. 15:19).

Preaching

Read also Romans 10:8-15

The message of the gospel has to do with certainties, and faith lays hold on these when they are preached, because faith comes by hearing the message as the word about Christ is declared (cf. Rom. 10:17). This was the preaching people heard when Epaphras came to them, and exactly the same gospel is still being preached throughout the world. The message is the same in every generation. Salvation and life are in Christ and Christ alone. He is the way, and the truth and the life. There is no other name given by which sinners can be saved and there is no other name or process or experience that is necessary (John 14:6; Acts 4:12). Note Paul's confidence in the gospel and in the preaching of it. He had seen its power in men's lives and he believed that wherever it is preached it will have the same effect. It will bring people to Christ, confirming them in their faith, building them up in character, conviction and service. He thrilled to the gospel.

Notice that there is no trace of envy of others. When Epaphras, whose ministry was richly blessed, came to Paul with such good news of the faith, hope and love of the Colossians, the apostle's heart rejoiced. Paul never believed that *he* was essential to the ongoing work of God and he was willing to serve and to suffer, counting it a privilege to have a share in God's work (Eph. 3:8). If his part was to write letters from the obscurity of prison in Rome and Epaphras' part was to be in the public eye preaching, then so be it, so long as Christ was preached (cf. Phil. 1:12-18). These two men would have encouraged each other. They were proud of the gospel, confident in it, and their greatest joy was to preach it.

The Holy Spirit

Read also John 16:7-15

There is great human and spiritual warmth in Paul's description of Epaphras. The great apostle was not slow to show how he felt about people and how he appreciated them. That is an example we do well to follow because it is all too easy to take people, their friendship and their ministry to us, for granted. Epaphras is described as a faithful minister or servant of Christ, and indeed to Paul as well as to the Colossians. In verse 8 Paul makes the only specific reference to the Holy Spirit in the whole of this epistle and this must surely be significant, especially since the context of the letter is that of spurious spirituality. What Paul seems to be affirming is that their coming to Christ, their growth in faith, hope, love and fellowship, and indeed the whole ministry of Epaphras which began the church in Colosse, all these were the work of the Holy Spirit. Love to Christ and to his people, and commitment to his work are the marks above all else of the presence and power of the Holy Spirit. The unmistakable evidence of the Spirit's presence and activity is a church where Jesus Christ the Son of God is the total focus of attention. The Holy Spirit's work is to testify to Christ (John 15:26).

These opening verses of the epistle are not merely introduction; they prepare for the correction and instruction Paul is about to give. He has emphasized the integrity of the ministry of Epaphras that had brought them to Christ. He has highlighted the new and growing life they found in Christ as preached by Epaphras. But we will see that these believers were being drawn away by teachers promising them 'knowledge' and 'special' ways of spiritual advance, and initiations into holiness through self-denials, all of which were false (2:20-23).

Lift up your eyes

Read also Ephesians 1:15-23

Paul now states specifically what he asks for the Colossians in his prayers. This passage (vv. 9-20) begins with Paul's prayer and develops into an exposition of the work and the person of Christ. This 'prison prayer' could well be read along with Paul's other prison prayers in Philippians 1:9-11; Ephesians 1:15-23; and 3:14-21. There is a grandeur and expansiveness in Paul's prayers as he intercedes for Christ's people and his church. Too many of our prayers never seem to get beyond, 'Lord, bless me and mine and my little world of friends and service.' Do we have any idea of just how far-reaching our service for Christ and the gospel could be if only we would recognize the reality and vitality of prayer?

Jesus commanded his disciples to pray that God would send labourers into a world where the harvest was ripe for reaping (Matt. 9:36-38; John 4:35). There are areas of the world about which we know little but we can pray for the increase of the church there. This is an ongoing work, as Paul makes plain, and he prays that the Christians will ever more fully enter into all that God has for them in Christ. Paul desires for them first of all knowledge of God's will. But this is not the kind of knowledge, secrets or techniques that initiate people into some special category of spiritual life. It is knowledge of God's will: not that we may be able to share all the mind of God but that we might have an ever fuller grasp of his purposes, his ways, his methods and his objectives. It is the business of knowing God, by learning what God is like; and that is acquired only by studying his Word. Read Joshua 1:8 and Romans 12:1-2.

Learn from Scripture

Read also Psalm 119:9-16

Paul wanted the believers to be filled to completeness by an ever-increasing knowledge of God's will. Perhaps he had in mind the need for 'the whole counsel of God' to be taught (Acts 20:27, NKJV) because we must not confine our concept of God and his will to our present limited understanding or experience. The will of God is spoken of elsewhere in terms of his sovereign predestination (Eph. 1:4-5), his revealing of his plans (Eph. 1:9-10), and his providential leading and ordering of our lives in relation to his work (Rom. 1:10).

This knowledge of God's will is not merely head knowledge and certainly not vague speculation or philosophizing. It is knowledge of the Scriptures in Spirit-given understanding. Paul is not speaking here of blinding flashes of revelation whereby we know at once what God is saying to us, although God reserves the right to work that way if he so chooses. Rather, we have to see here reference to the exercising of our faculties of thought and understanding whereby we come to have a clear grasp of what God wants us to do. Remember that Jesus promised the Holy Spirit would be our teacher to lead us into *all* the truth, not just our favourite themes (John 16:12-14). The Holy Spirit, who is the Spirit of truth, will enlighten our minds but never to displace Christ and never contrary to or independent of the Scriptures (Isa. 8:19-20). There is no doubt that God wants to open up to us wider and wider fields of understanding, showing us, as we are able to bear it, more of his plans for our lives and service. But this knowledge and understanding will never be total. There are things it is best we do not know about (Acts 1:7) and that is when we must simply trust God (Job 23:8-10).

Living for God

Read also John 15:1-5

The increase or filling of spiritual wisdom that Paul prays for is not to make people satisfied with themselves or think that they are superior to others. The aim is to enable them to live lives worthy of God, pleasing to him in all the different areas of life. It has to do with seeking and knowing the will of God before launching out into activity, and at the same time believing that God does and will guide us step by step. It is all wholly God-centred and very practical. The objective is to please God.

The desire to live in this way is the only real proof that our profession of faith and our claim to spirituality are real. Jesus said that those who love him *will* keep his commandments (John 14:15). The thing that must motivate us is not the desire for satisfaction or fulfilment, because that can lead to a very selective attitude to our participation in Christian service. For example, some people would not consider going to a prayer meeting because it does not appeal to them. Our business is to be obedient, to be worthy, and so to live that God will be pleased and glorified. That means we will be glad to serve in *every* good work, not just what we enjoy or what will give us prominence. That does not mean we accept every invitation or exhortation. We must seek assurance from God before deciding. Living like this, abiding in Christ, we will bear fruit (John 15:1-5). And in the process we will grow in grace, laying aside things that are essentially childish and irresponsible, and, as sons and daughters of God, become mature, grown up and dependable (1 Cor. 13:11-13; Heb. 5:11 - 6:3). Living to please God is to be our aim.

Inner power

Read also 2 Peter 1:3-9

This one verse should be linked with Ephesians 1:3,18-23 and Philippians 4:13,19. Paul has spoken of living a worthy life, pleasing God, bearing fruit and increasing in knowledge. By any standard that is a tremendous challenge. But it is within the reach of every believer because, in Christ, we have *in fact* been provided with all the inward strength and power needed. We do not have to go seeking for 'power' as if, having Christ, we still lacked something necessary for true Christian life. We must recognize that we have been given all things necessary for life and godliness (2 Peter 1:3-5). By faith we must appropriate the potential that is ours through the indwelling Spirit who *has been given* to us (Rom. 5:1-5).

The power we have is nothing less than the victorious, resurrection power of our Lord Jesus Christ, spoken of here as 'all power' and 'according to [or on the scale of] his glorious might'. The issue of this power working in us is spoken of in terms of endurance, patience and joy, and this leads on in the next verse to thanksgiving. These are the marks of the believer who is living in the power of the Holy Spirit. Paul is not speaking of a *display* of power, for the graces mentioned are quiet but sure. Always remember that inadequacy, insecurity and pride are much noisier than spirituality. Jesus was never noisy. He had no need to be, because he was sure of who he was and what he was doing (Isa. 42:1-4). The picture Paul paints is of life in Christ: a life not subject to nor qualified by the pressures of circumstances, nor by the activities of the devil. If we can grasp the potential we have, then, in Christ, all things really are possible.

The joy of the Lord

Read also Nehemiah 8:5-12

Look carefully at the 'graces' mentioned so that we will be able to recognize the marks of true Christian experience. Endurance is the spirit that persists and goes on in spite of all. It has more to do with 'slog' than obvious success. Patience is longsuffering, which is the opposite of impulsive retaliation. It is concerned with coping with frustrations and with people, and is the opposite of a hasty spirit. Joy is basically a quality of and an attitude to life rather than just excited emotion. It is not something we go looking for, nor something we try to produce or stir up within ourselves. We could almost say that joy is accidental because we find it or it registers within us as we go on our way concentrating on pleasing God and serving him. C. S. Lewis entitled his autobiography, *Surprised by Joy.*

Think of Jesus' words in John 15:10-11; Paul's words in Romans 15:13; Ezra and Nehemiah's words in Nehemiah 8:8-12; and David's words in Psalm 16:8-11. Joy comes when our minds and hearts are centred on God and we begin to realize how glorious God is and what a great salvation we have from him. It is this salvation Paul goes on to expound in verses 12-14 and he prefaces that exposition with the words 'giving thanks to the Father'.

It is often in the realm of thanksgiving that we are significantly lacking. It is so easy to take our salvation and all its blessings for granted. Imagine what life would be like without our Saviour and without all the benefits of fellowship with Christ and his people. But joy is not just enjoyment of blessings. Its setting is in the context of service and suffering. It was for the joy set before him that Jesus endured the cross, scorning the shame (Heb. 12:2).

A great salvation

Read also 1 John 3:1-3

Paul makes three great statements concerning the comprehensiveness of the salvation that is ours in Jesus Christ. We
have been qualified to share the inheritance of the saints;
we have been rescued from the dominion of darkness; and
we have been brought into the kingdom of God's Son. It is
on the basis of these facts that we live our lives, and begin
to see the ground we have for thanksgiving. This is good
and sure news, because it is all about what God has done
for us. God the Father Almighty has qualified us, in the
sense of giving us entitlement to a magnificent inheritance.
But we do not have to wait until we die to inherit. Paul is
speaking about life here and now. We have been given the
title deeds of salvation-life and we have the right to take
possession of all the blessings and benefits of that life here
and now. There is no room for doubt or uncertainty because it is God who has done this, and if God is for us, no
one can deny or even qualify our rights (Rom. 8:31-39). As
1 John 3:1-3 emphasizes, we need to behold (AV), to look
with real concentration on what God has given to us, what
he has made us and how he regards us.

Yet we must not think of this in a merely personal or
individual way. God has brought us into his blessing to
share it with all his people. This is the great corrective to
the loneliness and pointlessness of worldly life. Read what
Paul says in Ephesians 2:12-13,18-22 and savour the blessing of knowing that you *belong*. There is no need to feel
insecure or inferior. In Christ you are *family* whether you
are the youngest babe or the oldest grandparent. We belong, and we belong together and to each other. All that is
ours. This is our position and possession.

The Father's family

Read also Psalm 103:1-5,10-14

The assured sense of belonging, which is one aspect of salvation, stands over against the emptiness of life that people feel. So many are 'tired of living and scared of dying', feeling there is nothing now, nothing to come, nowhere to go and no point in anything. Over against the bleakness of unbelief stand the certainties of faith: a sure inheritance (1 Peter 1:3-5).

In a world where the ongoing effects of sin separate and isolate people from each other as well as from God, there is this reconciling effect of the gospel which brings us together in fellowship with a sense of security. It is the fellowship of the 'saints': those who belong to God through Jesus Christ, chosen by God and set apart for him (1 Peter 2:9). We are accepted for Jesus' sake, not because we deserve it. And this fellowship is in light, because God is light, and as we walk in the light with God and with each other the shadows of life begin to be dispelled.

We not only find relief for ourselves in the kindly light of God, we begin to see others more clearly and become far more aware of their good points and all they contribute, rather than aware of their faults and failures which once loomed so large. The best corrective to a critical spirit is a sense of the wonder and privilege granted to us in having a place at all in the family of God. When we begin to see and to feel that God is indeed a Father to us, a very loving, kind and considerate Father, we begin to see our responsibility. God has commanded that we love one another *as* he has loved us, with the same undeserved generosity, endless patience and understanding care (John 15:12).

Set free

Read also Romans 12:1-2

The salvation and fellowship that are ours in Christ are experienced in the real world in which evil is a fact and the person of evil, the devil, is a reality. If the theme of inheritance emphasized glorious destiny, today's theme is deliverance. This leads on in verses 13-14 to the thought of delight and enjoyment in the kingdom of God's beloved Son. When we speak of having been delivered, we recognize that apart from Christ we were in fact not free but in bondage. Ephesians 2:1-3 shows that our natural condition as sinners is one of spiritual death: bondage to what we are, what we have done and what we are becoming. In that condition, whether we are aware of it or not, we live in a world dominated and driven by the powers of evil (1 John 2:16; 5:19; Gal. 4:8; Eph. 6:10-12).

This is an alarming picture and we need to recognize how much we are influenced and conditioned by the 'powers of the world', such as advertising. Many of the religious programmes on radio and television are motivated by the philosophy of evolution, the denigration of the authority of Scripture, and the identification of the gospel with mere humanistic sociology. This is just one area of the battle for people's minds, and it is dangerously subtle. But Paul insists that there is no reason for Christian believers to be victims of atmosphere, culture or any other kind of pressure, because in and through the death and resurrection of Christ the whole kingdom of the devil has been overthrown and robbed of its power (Col. 2:15; Heb. 2:14-15; 1 John 3:8). The devil is a defeated foe. He no longer has any rights over us. We stand our ground, refusing all his intimidation and accusation. This is our right in Christ!

Amazing love

Read also Ephesians 3:14-21; Jeremiah 31:34

One of the great Easter hymns begins by affirming:

> Our Lord Christ hath risen! The tempter is foiled;
> His legions are scattered, his strongholds are spoiled.[3]

The hymn goes on to say that our great foe, Satan himself, is baffled; sin is conquered; and so is death, all because Christ Jesus is King. That great, conquering Jesus is identified and described as God's beloved Son who has established his kingdom, and has lifted us up and brought us into that kingdom with all its delights, assurances, privileges and enjoyments (Ps. 16:11). This is the context in which we now live our lives and we lack nothing that is necessary or good. God gives us all things in rich measure to enjoy (1 Tim. 6:17). He who gave us his Son will not be slow to give us all we need (Rom. 8:32). He has blessed us with every spiritual blessing and has given us all things necessary for life and godliness (Eph. 1:3; 2 Peter 1:3-4). All things are ours and we belong to Christ (1 Cor. 3:21-23).

Again and again in Paul's writings we are shown something of the sheer lavishness and generosity of God's goodness and grace, poured out on us and for us, all because of the love God has for his own beloved Son (Eph. 1:5-8; 3:14-21). The sheer scale of the phrase 'forgiveness of sins, in accordance with the riches of God's grace that he lavished on us' is almost too much to grasp. This is how God regards us and why he has brought us into the kingdom of his Son. Jesus himself knew we would find it hard to believe and that is why he prayed about it in John 17:23,26. Consider long and well the love God has for us (1 John 4:9-10).

Forgiveness

Read also 1 John 1:5 - 2:2

The words 'redemption' and 'forgiveness' bring this short passage to a climax. They are glorious words and demand response. With devotion and discernment Isaac Watts wrote:

> Love so amazing, so divine,
> Demands my soul, my life, my all.[4]

The Son of God, who loved us and gave himself for us (Gal. 2:20), took our sins in his own body and died to pay their price (1 Peter 3:18; Heb. 9:12; Gal. 4:4-5). The payment made to set us free was a costly one indeed (1 Peter 1:18-19), and we must never forget that. When, in Romans 3:24, Paul speaks of being justified freely by God's grace, he does so in the context of God setting forth his Son to be the atoning sacrifice for sin. Salvation may be free but it is not cheap, and we must remember this whenever we witness or preach.

The word redemption speaks of the sinner-slave being bought at a price from a tyrannical master and set gloriously free. In that salvation there is the forgiveness of *all* our sins. What a blessed relief (Ps. 32:1)! We have been loosed from our sins (Rev. 1:5). The apostles would often have seen Roman soldiers preparing for action, flicking the clasp that held their ceremonial cloak so that it would slip off, leaving them unhindered. They were 'loosed' from the cloak. When Bunyan's Pilgrim came to the cross, the burden of his sins fell from his back, rolling down the hill into the empty tomb, never to be seen again. This is forgiveness. There is pardon and cleansing, and all sins are put away so that God remembers them no more (Jer. 31:34). Never let the devil torment you about your past sins. They are dealt with. God does not want to hear about them any more.

The eternal Son

Read also John 1:1-14

If verses 12-14 expound the work of Christ, these verses detail the glorious person of Christ (see also Heb. 1:1-3). Jesus Christ has already been described as God's beloved Son, the object and focus of the total affection of the Father's heart. Now he is referred to as the executive of all God's plans and purposes. Both this passage and the one in Hebrews affirm that in every way and on every level Jesus Christ is Lord. Before time began, when the world was called into being, down the ages, and right through to the final consummation of history, Jesus Christ is Lord. This is the Jesus who said all power had been given to him (Matt. 28:18), and this is the Jesus who dwells in our hearts by faith. He is the full, perfect expression of all God is, as Jesus said to Philip in John 14:8-11. In the person of Jesus Christ God's glory and grace came into view.

> Veiled in flesh, the Godhead see;
> Hail the incarnate Deity,
> Pleased as Man with man to dwell,
> Jesus, our Immanuel.[5]

This Jesus was born in a stable! We need to think of the humility as well as the glory of God. How we should admire him, as we see him in fulness in his Son. Jesus is described as the 'first-born' of creation. We are thinking here of the eternal Sonship of Christ. God said, 'Let *us* make man in our image' (Gen. 1:26). 'In the beginning was the Word, and the Word was with God, and the Word was God' (John 1:1). No one has ever seen God but the only Son has made him known (John 1:18; 2 Cor. 4:6). Paul wants our horizon to be filled with Jesus.

Lord of creation

Read also Isaiah 40:21-26

These detailed verses, inspired by the Spirit of God, were originally written for the instruction and encouragement of new converts living in a godless society. We must not be unwilling to take time to study them carefully. Jesus is described now as Lord over all creation. Whether we think of creation as an act or a process, whether in seven days of twenty-four hours or days of 'geological eras', the fact is that Christ is the agent and instrument of bringing it into being *and* the end or objective for which it was created (John 1:3; Heb. 1:2; 11:3). The whole order of creation (and many scientists admit just how little they really know about it) has its completeness as well as its beginning in relation to Christ. Apart from Christ it has no meaning or significance and becomes a bewildering enigma and increasingly frightening. The defect in all mere scientific, sociological and political methods and philosophies is that they regard creation, people and history as ends in themselves.

With typical pride man tries to make himself the centre of creation; but this is not so. It is 'man in Christ' who is the key, as Romans 8:18-21 makes plain. There is a tremendous grandeur in the sweep of verse 16. All that can be seen and in measure understood, together with all that is real but remains invisible and beyond human capacity to understand, let alone control, together with 'thrones or powers or rulers or authorities' (whether good or evil), *all things* were created through him and for him. They are all for his use in carrying out the great and gracious purpose of the Father. This glorious Saviour is before all things and in him, by him, in relation to him, all things cohere and hold together. It should all make us very excited. Did we really know we had a Saviour like this?

Lord of providence

Read also 2 Peter 3:1-7

Christ the Lord of creation is also Christ the Lord of providence. The continuance of creation, all we mean by history, is not indiscriminate. It is carefully kept and maintained by the Word of God (2 Peter 3:1-7). Unbelief will never see this or admit it as a possibility. If Jesus is Lord of providence then there is progress right through history until he brings it to its planned fulfilment (1 Cor. 15:24-28). Because we believe this to be so, the world should have no terror for the Christian. There may be many things that baffle us and cause us suffering, and time and time again we will agree that God's ways are past finding out (Rom. 11:33). But we trust him. There is no reason why we should do otherwise. He is the God who gave his Son to die for us.

It is clear from the passage that Christ as Lord of creation is separate from what has been created but never absent from it. He allows evil, but is never implicated in it. He works through natural processes, which means that time is on his side and he never needs to hurry. As Lord, he is also free to work outside, apart from and in contradiction of natural laws. Miracles are no problem. The Lord of creation is not controlled by what he has created. He pursues throughout history his mighty plan of redemption, and faith must learn to discern and to concentrate on what God is doing, rather than be deceived and frightened by what men and devils seem able to do. Think of the significant interpretation of history we are given in such verses as Acts 2:22-24; 4:23-28; and Genesis 50:15-21. Even the secular poets at times see this truth. Shakespeare's Hamlet says, 'There is a divinity that shapes our ends, rough hew them how we will.'[6]

Lord of history

Read also Revelation 5:1-7

We must now think of the Lord of providence in a personal way. We tend to forget the fact that there is a hand that guides and a heart that plans (Ps. 31:15), and as a result we lose a great deal of peace and encouragement. God knows his children are often not aware of his presence and activity (Isa. 45:5,15; Hos. 11:1-3). In Psalm 23:1 the Lord of providence is my shepherd who leads, guides and guards. He keeps me as the apple of his eye and protects me (Ps. 17:8). This gracious and glorious Lord assures me that my heavenly Father knows what I need (Matt. 6:32), and he also reassures me when things happen, or fail to happen and cause me confusion (John 13:7; 16:12). He knows the way I take (Job 23:10) and his promises stand sure and good (Isa. 41:10; 43:1-2).

However, lest we become too preoccupied with our own little world of experience, consider the Lord of providence in universal terms and see again the immense comfort and assurance this gives. The times and seasons are in his power (Acts 1:7). The rise and fall of governments and empires are also in his power and his alone, no matter what appearances may otherwise suggest (Dan. 4:17,35). The programme of history is timed to a moment (Rev. 9:15; 10:6) and the final victory is never in doubt (1 Cor. 15:22-28). When we see the intrigues of nations and the emergence of clear and deliberate antichrist power and policy, we must look to the fact of sovereign providence whereby even the devil himself is compelled to serve God's purpose (Rev. 17:17). God's plans and purposes are never for a moment in doubt. The executor is none other than our glorious Lord and Saviour Jesus Christ who is pictured in Revelation 5:1-7 with the perfect plan in his hand.

Lord of the church

Read also Revelation 1:4-20

In verse 18 Christ is declared to be Lord of the church. Imagine what this must have meant to the small group of believers in the pagan city of Colosse, feeling things were against them, battling hard and perhaps tempted to despair. This glorious Christ, the eternal, pre-existent one, the beloved Son of God, the mighty Victor, is the head of the church, which is his body. This means not only that the church is united to Christ, who is its head, but also that the church is the means whereby all that Christ is and wills to do is expressed in the world. The church is vitalized by Christ's presence, energized by his power, directed and controlled by his wisdom and is his instrument in the world for carrying out his work on a scale far vaster than just in one locality.

What an inspiration and encouragement this truth must have been to the Christians in Colosse, and is to us now in our situation. Whatever else we are, we are not irrelevant nor impotent, nor are we in any sense required to act on our own. Christ is the only head of the church and he is leading, disciplining and perfecting the whole body and its activity. At times the visible church may be harassed, scattered, assailed, submerged and obscured. But the body of Christ cannot die. This is the glory of the doctrine of the church and it is sad that present-day individualism has clouded this truth. We are not divided. We are one body in Christ, and Christ in all his glory is present in his church, holding it and all its aspects in the right hand of his power. This was a message the Colossians needed to hear (Rev. 1:4-20).

The all-sufficient Christ

Read also Hebrews 1:1-3

We see Christ now as the Lord of redemption. God the Father is the subject of the sentence and this takes us right into the eternal counsels of God in his perfect plan and purpose for salvation. At the heart of the eternal plan, embodying every aspect of it, there stands Christ. It was the Father's will that all fulness should dwell in his Son, who stands unique and pre-eminent; the Son in whom the Father is ever well pleased. The picture in Revelation 5:6 shows the Lamb slain at the heart of God's eternal throne. Apostolic preaching declared, 'Salvation is found in no one else...' (Acts 4:12). The glorious statement in Philippians 2:8-11 declares that God has given to this same Jesus, crucified and risen, the name above every name. The whole plan of salvation, in all its aspects, is found perfectly in Jesus Christ. All the fulness of God — all God is, says and has to give — is in Christ. He is God's final and complete 'word' to the world (Heb. 1:1-3), and out of his fulness (which is never diminished) we receive grace upon grace to meet our every need (John 1:16).

This Jesus is the one Mediator between God and man (1 Tim. 2:5) and we need no other in order to come to God and prove the glorious salvation which God has worked for us through him. If we link verse 19 with 2:9-10 we can say that if all the fulness of God is in Christ, and we have Christ, then we who have believed have *now* in unqualified measure all that there is to have in terms of salvation and life. This was a message much needed in Colosse, where prevailing philosophy spoke of a range of intermediaries to be dealt with if men would deal with God.

It is finished

Read also Hebrews 9:11-14,24-26

The affirmations that all 'fulness' is in Christ and that an undivided Christ is in us who believe by the Holy Spirit (Rom. 8:9-11) are necessary correctives to a variety of hazy and emotional ideas about salvation and victorious Christian living. Paul's statement in verse 20 is also necessary for clear thinking. It concerns the fact of a once-for-all, never-to-be-repeated, decisive act by God whereby, through Jesus Christ, he made peace through the atoning death of the cross. The only way to understand the cross is to see that God was in Christ reconciling the world to himself (2 Cor. 5:19). It was God who ordained that Christ should be made sin for us (2 Cor. 5:21). It was God who laid on Christ the iniquity of us all (Isa. 53:4-6). It was God who delivered him up to the death of the cross (Rom. 8:32). And when Christ died, once for all, he made full atonement for sin and secured for us eternal redemption (Heb. 9:11-14, 24-26).

Peace with God was made by virtue of the shedding of the blood of the Son as a sacrifice for sin, paying its price and meeting its judgement in full. We must see that our salvation rests in a peace that God has made. In that peace we are reconciled to God, by God himself, so that there is no longer any condemnation or separation, and we are in harmonious fellowship with him. This is both peace and joy (Rom. 5:1-2; 8:1,35-39) and it opens the door to limitless possibility and thrill as we begin to see that our personal salvation is part of something far greater than our limited experience. Indeed, it is something that will not be seen in full measure until the glory of the eternal world.

Final victory

Read also Revelation 21:1-5

Grasp the comprehensiveness of Paul's concept of redemption. The reconciliation God accomplished is not limited to humanity, but applies to the whole order of creation and created beings, whether on earth or in heaven. The same vast plan is spoken of in Ephesians 1:7-10. Note however that Paul does not say or even suggest that all men and women will be saved. That would be contrary to his teaching elsewhere and a contradiction of the words of Jesus who warned that persistent unbelief would result in people dying in their sins (John 8:21,24). In Colossians Paul is still dealing with the completeness of the plan of God and that includes the redemption of the natural order of creation, which was dragged down into bondage by the fall of man. In Romans 8:19-22 Paul links the final deliverance of creation to the revelation of the sons of God, the complete gathering in of the redeemed.

When Paul says that things in heaven are also included in this great reconciliation it is difficult to know exactly what he is referring to. He may be saying that whatever 'orders' of supernatural beings there may be, God deals with them all only on the basis of the great redemption that is in Christ. This does not mean that all the principalities and powers in heavenly places (Eph. 6:10-12) will finally be reconciled to God, for that would suggest the salvation of Satan and his evil hosts who are destined for destruction (Matt. 25:41). There are beings and powers who will be subdued not saved (1 Cor. 15:24) and not all who bow to the Lordship of Christ will do so willingly. Paul emphasizes that God's perfect plan, in Christ, will not be frustrated and the end will be a new order of existence from which all alien influences will be banished for ever (Rev. 21:1-5).

A hopeless state

Read also Ephesians 2:1-5,12

Against the glorious background of a cosmic plan of redemption Paul now speaks to the Colossians about their
personal salvation. He reminds them vividly of what they
had been in relation to God apart from Christ. They were
by nature estranged from God, alienated from him, separated from his presence, enemies not friends. This alienation was not a superficial one caused by certain actions; it
involved their minds, the deepest part of their beings, their
essential disposition. This inward rebellion and enmity
towards God had manifested itself in evil actions. It was
because they were sinners by nature that they manifested
in their lives evil deeds that were contrary to God. As a
result they were under his wrath and condemnation (Rom.
1:18; 3:9,19). Paul states the same truth in Ephesians 2:1-
3,12, where he tells sinners the facts about themselves: they
are Christless, stateless, friendless, hopeless and godless.
This is what it means to be a sinner, separated from God. It
is a condition of total hopelessness, total inability to better
your condition, and total bondage.

Also in the passage in Ephesians Paul speaks of living
under the control of the spirit of disobedience and at the
same time being driven by the desires of body and mind.
Whatever else we are and have, if we are apart from Jesus
Christ, we have neither freedom nor hope. It is only when
we begin to try to be good, to resist the pressures of both
worldliness and our own fallen human nature, that we begin
to realize that unless someone from outside ourselves comes
to our aid we will remain victims and prisoners, under the
power of sin. This is the truth whether we feel it to be so or
not. But God acted for the salvation of sinners (Eph. 2:4-
10).

Reconciliation

Read also 1 Corinthians 12:14-27

The difference salvation makes is total. Sinners who were outside are brought inside, reconciled to God and accepted as full and valid members of his household (Eph. 2:13,19-22). All this happened to the Colossians (and to us who believe) through the death of Christ, the Son of God, who took our fleshly nature, lived our life, was tempted just as we are yet without sin, and died for us. When we read in Scripture that the eternal Word of God became flesh (John 1:14) we must be clear that this was not just a story but reality. He became a real man, as human as we are (Heb. 2:14-18; 4:14-16).

Paul has already spoken of peace through the blood of the cross (v. 20) and now speaks of peace by Christ's physical body (v. 22). This confirms to the Colossians the reality of the incarnation. It emphasizes the fact that he was born to *die*. There may also be in Paul's mind some connection in thought between 'in his body' and 'the body, the church' (v. 18). A great emphasis in Paul's writings is the description of the believer as being 'in Christ'. If then we are in Christ, we are in his body, which is the church. This means we are together in him as members of his body, belonging and functioning together, with Christ as the head. We are members one of another; we belong; we have function and significance, working together in harmony, complementing each other. Read more of this in 1 Corinthians 12:12-20 and remember that the reality of our reconciliation to God is made manifest in the life and fellowship of the church. If we are the kind of people who do not get on with anyone, who do not belong to any church, or who disrupt and dislocate a fellowship, then we should examine our profession of faith; and our understanding of reconciliation.

Stand firm in faith

Read also Hebrews 10:32-39

God's objective in this marvellous work of salvation and reconciliation is to present us together in his presence in flawless perfection, faultless and stainless. The New Testament is full of such glorious intentions and anticipations. Consider the passages in Ephesians 5:25-27; 2 Corinthians 3:18; 1 John 3:1-5; and Jude 24. The end makes all the cost worthwhile and we should be utterly amazed at the sheer dimension of God's plans for us. We have a destiny of glory. In that glory no finger of reproach will ever be pointed at us; not just because it is God who justifies (Rom. 8:31-34); not just because the devil, the accuser, has been banished to his own terrible place (Matt. 25:41); but because God's perfect work in us has been brought to completion to the praise of his glorious grace (Eph. 1:6; 2:7). Cleansed of every spot and stain of sin we shall be able to stand before God; perhaps then we will understand the price that was paid for our salvation and realize at last just how much we owe our Saviour.

This glorious and assured prospect must never make us careless or complacent. We must continue in the faith. We must not go back (Gal. 1:6-9; Heb. 10:32-39). We must build ourselves up in our faith (Jude 20), desiring both the milk and the meat of God's Word (1 Peter 2:1-2; Heb. 5:11-14). We must fight the good fight of faith if we are to lay hold on eternal life (1 Tim. 6:12). There is no escape from the battle and, after the first flush of spiritual enthusiasm, it is the grace of perseverance that confirms the validity of our spiritual experience.

Conflict and victory

Read also Romans 5:1-5

To begin to understand this deep and mysterious verse we need to look back to verse 23 where Paul was teaching the believers that in the experience of the individual and the church there is the need both to stand firm and to go on. This will mean conflict. But this is not in any sense a denial of the total victory of Christ. In Christian experience conflict and victory go together, and claiming and realizing Christ's victory in our lives brings us into what Paul elsewhere calls the fellowship of his sufferings (Phil. 3:7-11).

It seems that some false teachers in Colosse were preaching a 'spirituality' that would lead to a 'higher' kind of experience in which battles became a thing of the past. This is still being preached today, and people look for experiences that will lead them into a life of some kind of euphoric victory or fulness in which they will not have any more problems. This is *not* the biblical picture of Christian life and experience, nor is it the way of fruitful and continuing service. Paul is seeking to shift the eyes of the Colossians away from preoccupation with their own spiritual experience to the glorious picture of the worldwide preaching of the gospel. It is when we begin to realize what a vast and marvellous dimension of Christian work we are involved in, that we begin to be able to interpret, understand and cope with the rigours and demands of ongoing Christian life and service. Part of that process is our progressive sanctification, and when we see this, instead of complaining about difficulties and seeking to escape from them, we begin to understand God's ways with us, and with others through us. This is the theme of verse 24. In order to grapple with the truth of this one verse, consider James 1:2-4; and 1 Peter 1:6-9; 4:1,12-14.

121

Understand your battles

Read also Philippians 3:7-11

There is no suggestion whatever that there is anything lacking in the saving death of our Lord Jesus Christ. He himself declared from the cross, 'It is finished.' Paul has already spoken of Christ as the head of the church (v. 18), and the head and the body belong together. Now Paul brings together in a very positive way his personal battles and sufferings as a minister, the continuing experience of the Colossian believers, the life and work of the church throughout the world, and the afflictions or sufferings of Christ. He insists that individual and corporate experiences are not to be separated. The struggles of one believer are part of the life, work and progress of the congregation of which he or she is a member. The battles being worked out in the service of the gospel in one congregation are part of, and linked to, the ongoing work of other fellowships for which they pray. We are in it together and we must not interpret our costly struggles only in relation to our own personal experience.

The battles and struggles we go through *in Christ* have significance in places and among people with whom we have no direct contact at all. Paul had never been to Colosse, but he sees his sufferings in various places as being, in some mysterious but glorious way, part of the ongoing work of Christ the Suffering Servant. It means in practical terms that, as we seek to stand in Christ, to grow in grace, to resist the devil (all of which are part of the ongoing process of our personal sanctification), our battles are a vital part of the sovereign purpose of God through Jesus Christ whereby sinners are saved and added to the church. This is the fellowship of sufferings whereby Christ's saving victory is worked out in history.

The privilege of suffering

Read also Acts 9:1-6,16

This verse teaches us what a great privilege has been granted to us. We who believe are allocated, as we are able to bear it, a share in the costly travail whereby salvation comes to men and women all over the world. The context of this verse is the life, work and witness of Christ's church and it is clear that Christ continues to suffer in his members (Acts 9:4-5,15-16) as they suffer in fellowship with him. Remember that right at the start of the apostolic church the believers rejoiced that they were counted worthy of suffering for the sake of Christ (Acts 5:40-42). Read quickly through this sequence of references to see just how often this theme is emphasized in Scripture: Romans 8:17; 2 Corinthians 1:5-7; 4:8-12; Philippians 1:27-30; 3:10; 1 Peter 2:21. Keep clearly in mind that all over the world the work of salvation is still going on, and will go on, until its perfect end. Since we are in Christ, and Christ is in us by his Holy Spirit, it is inevitable that we should experience at least something of his longings for a lost world; his yearning for the salvation of sinners; and something of the costly shame and rejection he suffered when he went so willingly to the cross.

There will be times when we simply do not understand why we must go through deep darkness, and our suffering will seem pointless. But even our Saviour, in the midst of darkness, struggle and suffering on the cross, asked, 'Why?' The fellowship of his sufferings, whether in the struggles of sanctification, the battles of active service, or in the baffling experiences we all suffer as part of the fallen human race, is costly evangelism. In the words of the hymn by Horatius Bonar: 'It is the way the Master went, should not the servant tread it still?'[7]

Glorious service

Read also Ephesians 3:2-11

Paul moves from the theme of costly service in the gospel to that of the immense privilege of being a minister of Christ's church. The word used for 'minister' is literally 'deacon' and signifies a working servant. It is the privilege of labour rather than position and recognition that Paul emphasizes. At the same time he affirms that this ministry was given to him as a commission from God, a stewardship of the gospel, especially in relation to the Gentiles, and that included the Colossians (Acts 9:15; 22:21; 1 Cor. 9:16-18). The heart of that commission was to make the Word of God fully known, and the whole of Paul's life was dedicated to that end, as he made plain in his farewell address to the elders at Ephesus (Acts 20:17-27). Paul testified that he kept back nothing that was profitable. There is a continuing temptation, often in order to be popular, to qualify the costly substance of the gospel message or to proclaim it in such an attractive way that the hearers are able to escape the challenge (1 Cor. 1:17).

When Paul speaks of 'mystery', he is referring to something God has now revealed; not just God's plan of redemption, but the sheer dimension of the gathering of multitudes of Gentiles from all over the world, making of Jew and Gentile one glorious church in which race, background and culture are swallowed up. The glory of God's saving purposes was not fully known to earlier generations or even to angelic beings, as Peter makes plain (1 Peter 1:10-12). This teaches us that we, in our turn, may well never realize the full extent or significance of the work we are doing, because it is essentially for the future. That should be a great encouragement to those who feel they are seeing little 'result' for their costly labours.

Glory

Read also 2 Peter 1:16-18

Read Ephesians 3:7-13 and note words such as 'unsearchable', 'intent' and 'manifold wisdom'. Then consider Ephesians 3:20-21, referring to the generations of history; Ephesians 2:7; and 3:10, which seem to refer to the ages of eternity. What a glorious revelation and demonstration of God's grace and glory there will be ultimately, world without end. We have not begun to grasp the glory of the purposes of God, which evokes such doxologies as we have in the book of Revelation (Rev. 4:11; 5:13; 7:12). All this majestic glory (2 Peter 1:16-18) is a sure and guaranteed hope (Rom. 5:1-2). The fact that Christ is in us and among us is our assurance. Think of the wonderful words of Christ in Revelation 3:20. He comes in to dwell, not as a passing visitor but as a permanent guest, making his home in us and with us. We need to remember, more than we do, that it is the glorious Christ who lives in our hearts, and he will not leave his work of salvation incomplete. What he began he will bring to perfection (Phil. 1:6). Those who are justified in Christ are also glorified, according to Paul's magnificent statement in Romans 8:30; or as Toplady's hymn affirms:

> More happy, but not more secure,
> The glorified spirits in heaven.[8]

Ponder in a spirit of worship the words 'Christ in you'. Why should the glorious one be willing to live in such poor surroundings as our sinful hearts, and our small congregations, so marked with imperfections? Of course, when he first came to earth, a stable was enough. That is the kind of Saviour he is. And he plans to make both ourselves and his church spotless and perfect (Eph. 5:26-27).

Christ the focus

Read also Acts 20:17-24; 2 Timothy 4:6-8

There is something stirring about Paul's words, 'We proclaim him'. For Paul, the real business of preaching involved the preacher getting out of the way so that Christ alone might be seen (2 Cor. 4:5). Whatever other preachers and teachers proclaimed as their message, Paul presented Christ as the one and only all-sufficient Saviour, the life and hope of his people. But Paul's gospel had also an element of challenge (Acts 20:21). There was need for repentance and for guarding against sin and any kind of presumption. There was also the teaching of the truths of God's Word so that believers would understand more fully all they had been given in Christ. In a wicked world, riddled with false philosophies and religions, Christians need to know what they believe and on what grounds they believe. This is one reason why we need to study Colossians in such detail. These words would not have been given by God if they had not been necessary for us.

'With all wisdom' seems to refer to the application of all God's truth to the practical business of living lives that please God. It is *all* wisdom; not a few selected special truths to the exclusion of all else. The objective which calls for all Paul's God-given energy, and to which he is prepared to work with every fibre of his being, is to present all believers mature in Christ. He does not merely want to have something worthwhile to show when his work is done; but desires that the fruit of his ministry will be worthy of God and to the glory of his name (1 Thess. 2:19-20; 5:23-24; 1 John 2:28). How would we feel if, after years of Christian life sitting under rich ministry, we stood finally before the Saviour still spiritual babies with little or no service rendered to him who gave all for us? What a waste!

Prayer

Read also Ephesians 6:18-20

Paul has spoken of his ministry in terms of toiling, striving and great effort in the strength of that inward energy which is, of course, supplied by the Holy Spirit. The word 'struggling' (1:29; 2:1) is the word used of contestants in the arena giving every effort and fighting off fatigue and faintness. The AV uses the word 'striving' in 1:29 and translates the same word 'conflict' in 2:1. Different translations help to convey something of the essential cost of the great missionary's earnest care for the Colossians and his desire that they might be all that they should be and could be for Christ. Paul was aware of subtle influences and distractions endangering the faith of the believers in Colosse. But what could he do about this situation? He could not go to Colosse because he was in prison. He was writing to them to teach them, but underlying all his ministry and care there were his prayers. Before we consider the detail of his prayers we need to recognize that prayer was at the heart of his whole life. We see this in all his letters. He was constantly asking his fellow believers to pray for him, for the work, and for the preaching of the gospel.

It is right that we remind ourselves of Paul's emphasis on prayer because many evangelical Christians are willing to engage in almost any and every kind of Christian work *except* prayer. Read Ephesians 6:18-20; Colossians 4:2-4; and 2 Thessalonians 3:1-2. This is Christian service that cannot be hindered by circumstances, health, opposition or prison doors. The way to God's throne is always open for us in the name of Jesus. Why do we not use it more often?

Unity

Read also Romans 12:16-18; Ephesians 4:1-3

Paul reminded the Colossians that many others had an equal right to a share in his love and prayers (v. 1). The burden of his care and prayer is clear. If they were to face up to the influences that were distorting and hindering the gospel and causing them to be led astray from faith and service, then they needed to be encouraged and to find fresh heart and conviction. This would only occur if they were united in love. Both the AV and RSV translate the word 'united' as 'knit together'. This is a vivid illustration of true Christian fellowship. The individual strands are woven together into one united pattern. 'Threads' that stick out spoil the whole effect, as do 'dropped stitches' and 'wrong tension'. And, of course, there is a 'knitter'; and he is God, the Holy Spirit, whose great concern is always to 'keep the unity of the Spirit through the bond of peace' (Eph. 4:1-3; Rom. 12:16-18). Read Ephesians 4:25-32 and remember that when by word, action or lack of action, we do anything to cause dissension in the fellowship, we grieve the Holy Spirit.

Perhaps Paul is thinking here of being knit together by common instruction, experience and service. There is no doubt that when we work together and go through battles together the bond of fellowship becomes stronger and sweeter. In the whole matter of growing in grace to spiritual maturity it is in fellowship with others that we learn. It is within the fellowship that our growth in understanding and assurance becomes evident and there comes with this an increase in peace. The influence of false teachers in Colosse was having the opposite effect. There was restlessness and uncertainty, and when that is being caused by some who claim to be 'extra' spiritual or to have 'higher' knowledge, we can be sure we are dealing with something sinister.

True knowledge

Read also 2 Peter 1:1-9

False teaching very often centres on adding to Christ, suggesting that something more is needed for true salvation. Paul is concerned to do two things. Firstly, he is setting the believers on guard against those who would intellectualize the Christian faith as if knowledge were an end in itself. Secondly, he is emphasizing that a true grasp of the spiritual revelation of the gospel can never be attained apart from the growth of brotherly love within the fellowship of the church. At the end of verse 2 the phrase, 'the mystery of God, namely, Christ', is used by Paul to restrain any tendencies to depart into speculative philosophy with regard to spiritual things. The 'knowledge' we need has been revealed in Jesus Christ, who himself is 'the way and the truth and the life' (John 14:6). All advance in knowledge is gained by an ever deeper searching into the treasure store of Scripture with the help of the Holy Spirit, whose function is to take the things of Christ and reveal them to us (John 16:14-15).

Because the treasures are hidden (v. 3) there needs to be a single-minded earnestness to seek them out. It is not just knowledge that is spoken of, but wisdom. It is possible to become a veritable human encyclopaedia of information about the Scriptures without ever expressing the truth in human grace and love. If that is so, in spite of all their knowledge, such people remain unable to minister grace and encouragement to others. Such persons are seldom found in the place of prayer, perhaps because they feel they are above such a thing, or perhaps because they simply have no interest in such costly, self-denying exercises.

False influences

Read also Matthew 7:15-23

This one verse, linked with other Scriptures, shows clearly that throughout biblical history, in Old Testament and New Testament alike, God's people have had to guard against false teachers and spurious influences. This is true in our own day and we must ensure we do not become discouraged and demoralized when we hear of so many voices inside and outside the church confusing, qualifying and denying the substance of the faith. This is nothing new. We must remember that God watches over his own word to fulfil it (Jer. 1:12, RSV); and he has declared that it will not return empty but will accomplish what it has been sent to do (Isa. 55:10-11). It is God who stands guard over his church like a wall of fire (Zech. 2:5) and, as he builds his church, the gates of hell cannot and will not prevail (Matt. 16:18).

It is from this vantage point of assurance that we prepare to deal with any and all of the spurious messengers who claim to be sent by God for our blessing, but who are in fact agents of Satan to deceive us. We must not be taken in by appearances, eloquence or even signs and wonders, because the devil can speak well (as he did in the Garden of Eden) and he can also work miracles. Consider 2 Corinthians 11:13-15; Matthew 7:21-23; Philippians 3:17-19; 1 Timothy 4:1-3; 2 Peter 2:1-3; and 1 John 4:1; which are only a few of many references on this point and do not include any from the Old Testament. How we need to be on guard against strong personalities and powerful emotional persuasion. Always consider where these influences are leading. If they make you separate from the fellowship and the ministry under which you have been nurtured in Christ, a ministry where the Word of God has been dealt with in its full content and consistency, then beware.

Guard the gospel

Read also 2 Timothy 1:13-14; 4:1-5

Although Paul is concerned about the dangers threatening the new believers, he also recognizes what is good, and he commends them for their good order and the firmness of their faith in Christ. The warmth with which he writes (v. 5) must have encouraged them, especially when it came from one who had only heard about them. The reference to good order reminds us of the dangers of disorder and this must be recognized by those preoccupied with informality in the life of the church.

When Paul writes of the faith in which they were taught (v. 7) we have a clear indication that there was already an accepted body of doctrinal truth adhered to by all the churches. This was necessary so that there would be a guarantee of the continuity and integrity of the Christian message. It is significant that in our generation there is a distaste for any insistence upon a doctrinal basis and this has led to a degree of real confusion about what the gospel is. We must take very seriously the warning in Jude 3-4 over denials of the faith stirring inside the church. If faith is not securely grounded in the systematic doctrines of Scripture, false teachers will have an open door for their destructive work. All sorts of secondary matters will be so emphasized that they will become a focus of distraction, and division and criticism will take the place of thankfulness. It is little wonder that when Paul wrote to the Galatians he expressed shock that some had departed from the faith so soon and insisted that there are matters of fundamental truth about which there can be no disagreement (Gal. 1:6-9). The young minister Timothy was urged to guard the gospel (2 Tim. 1:13-14; 4:1-5). To do that, are we prepared to study hard so that we know our Bibles?

A great salvation

Read also John 15:1-5

Some talk too easily about faith in Christ and receiving Christ, and tend to think of conversion as a terminus rather than a beginning. In the New Testament it is not so. In Romans 5:1-5 faith is linked with trials and sufferings which produce character. In 2 Corinthians 4:7-12 faith leads to costly service. In 2 Peter 1:3-11 the call to supplement or add to our faith seems to emphasize that God has provided or implanted life in all its potential and we are to develop or cultivate or nourish that 'seed' life so that it will grow to fulness.

The same thoughts of growth and progress are evident in these verses here. Paul goes on to develop the thought from faith in Christ (v. 5) to having received Christ as Lord (v. 6). Then he speaks of living 'in Christ' (a theme he deals with later). This leads on to thinking of Christ as the 'soil' into which our roots go down, drawing life from and growing in him (cf. John 15:1-5). Then Christ is referred to as a secure foundation on which our lives are being built up, giving us both solidity and permanence. The whole passage compels us to enlarge our thinking about what the Christian life is and can be and, says Paul, these converts had been taught this right from the start. It was not a narrow gospel confined to 'making a decision' that was preached, but rather fulness of life in Jesus Christ. When we begin to grasp what we have been given in Christ, we begin to see the possibilities of this truly great salvation we have. We need to recover our sense of wonder at the great thing God has done for us. Are we so aware of what we have in Christ that, like the Colossians, our hearts are overflowing with thanksgiving?

Dangers

Read also 2 Peter 1:16-21

The phrase 'See to it', which introduces these verses, sounds a note of warning about the danger of false teachers. Although Paul does not name any person or group of people it seems that he had been informed by Epaphras about exactly what was going on in Colosse and who was behind it. He is in fact challenging the motives of the false teachers and contradicting their teaching. He describes them as trapping the Christian believers, drawing them into their clutches, presumably so that they might increase their own following and so become powerful figures on the religious scene.

There are still those who target young converts, pressurizing them to believe and to do various things in order to become 'really spiritual', or 'fully blessed', or 'totally consecrated', or 'filled, baptized, sealed with the Spirit'. Such people seldom do any real evangelistic work of their own among those with no church connection. Instead they operate like spiritual wolves preying on someone else's flock. Note how Paul describes these false teachers. He does not refer to anything ugly or depraved. The Christians were not being tempted to obvious sinfulness but were being influenced in a far more subtle way. We are in the realm of words and ideas which Paul describes as empty and false philosophy. But the Christian faith is not built on speculation; it is based on revealed facts. God has spoken fully and finally and on this we stand (Heb. 1:1-2; 2 Peter 1:16-21). Religious traditions as well as secular attitudes are powerful influences and can so easily replace the message of the gospel. Jesus tackled this problem head on, as he made so clear in his words to the religious leaders of that day. His words were powerful and uncompromising (Matt. 15:1-9).

Wrong principles

Read also Deuteronomy 18:9-13

History tells of a culture of 'mysteries' and 'secret initiations' which was rife in the pagan society of Colosse. It was from this background and these influences that the believers had been brought to Christ. They had to learn that such influences, attitudes and practices must not be allowed to direct or control their Christian lives. Paul refers to the 'basic principles of this world', 'the elemental spirits of the universe' (RSV), the 'rudiments' or the 'elements' of the world (AV). He may be referring here simply to the way the world thinks and speculates, a pattern of thought in which the God of Christian revelation is totally excluded (Ps. 10:4). This attitude to God is one reason why we must not be conformed to the thinking of the world (Rom. 12:2).

There is no suggestion at all that Paul despises education. Nor does he deny the need to grapple mentally with the problems and experiences of life. But he insists that we think on right principles, starting from reliable historical truths and not from mere speculation. He may also be thinking of a connection between the various rites practised in Colosse and the activities of evil spirits. He speaks in 1 Corinthians 10:20 of the fact that idolatrous worship is not simple or innocent. If we take 1 John 5:19 and Ephesians 6:10-12 seriously, we can see there some reference to the 'elemental spirits of the universe' and how they impinge on human experience, especially before we came to know the Saviour (Eph. 2:2). When we consider the interest today in 'star signs' and the occult, even among children, with ouija boards; when we see how people become addicted to hallucinatory drugs; then we realize that Paul's warnings must still be taken seriously.

Complete in Christ

Read also 1 Corinthians 2:1-9

In his commentary on Colossians F. F. Bruce entitles verses 8-15, 'Christ is all — and all you need'. Paul contrasts the false philosophy with the fact that the whole of a perfect, complete and glorious salvation is to be found in Christ and in him alone. Anything that denies or distracts from Christ is suspect. This is how we too can deal with the peddlers of religion who come to our doors. What do they say about the person of Christ? What do they say about his full and perfect atonement for sin? And what do they say about the Bible as God's inspired and authoritative written revelation of himself and his salvation?

The message concerning this Jesus is not manufactured by the wisdom of this age (1 Cor. 2:6-8). It is revealed in and given by Jesus Christ in whom all fulness dwells. If we have Christ, then we have everything. All fulness resides in Jesus; it is imparted by him; and it is ours by virtue of our union with him. This means we have come to fulness of life in him and in him alone. This Jesus, in whom we are complete, is the head over all rule and authority, in whatever form these rulers and authorities appear in the human situation and in whatever realm, earthly or heavenly, they operate. Since we have this Jesus there is nothing we lack and nothing we need to fear. We have, as an old tract used to say, 'Safety, Certainty and Enjoyment'. We must not forget the enjoyment. It is easy to focus on the battle and the cost, but the truth is that as we set ourselves, in Christ, to glorify God we do in fact begin to enjoy him both now and in anticipation of the world to come. Any persons, influences or doctrines that seek to steal from us our full treasure in Christ have to be opposed and exposed, and this is what Paul is doing.

New creatures in Christ

Read also Romans 6:1-11

We have been given fulness of life in Christ (v. 10). Now Paul elaborates on this new life that is ours whereby we become partakers of the divine nature (2 Peter 1:3-4). Paul, assuming the Colossians knew something about Jewish religious practice, uses as illustration the rite of circumcision. The emphasis is not on the physical act but the spiritual significance: a cutting off and a putting away of the sinful nature, the whole of our carnal 'Adam' nature; not the physical act administered by man but the spiritual 'surgery' carried out by God (Deut. 30:6). Circumcision was a sign, just as baptism is a sign. It is not the mechanics or method of administering the sign that are important, but its meaning with regard to the activity of God. *The Tyndale Commentary* by H. M. Carson has an illuminating two pages on these verses that are well worth close study but too detailed to quote here.

The 'old nature', in its full potential geared to rebellion against God and exercising dominion over natural man, has been dealt with and stripped away. But it has not ceased to exist. It will always try to assert itself. The believer must realize what God has done and take his stand on that, repudiating and refusing all the clamour of the old nature. This radical change in our nature has been worked by God. The sinner is accepted in Christ. The new life has been born by the Spirit through the Son. The believer is a new creation. This is Paul's theme also in Romans 6:1-11. We need to recognize what God has done for us and made us in Christ. It is only as we grasp this truth that we can begin to prove his power in the practicalities of living the Christian life. We do not go looking for an 'experience' to make us new creatures. We *are* new creatures in Christ (2 Cor. 5:17).

Raised from the dead

Read also Ephesians 1:15-21

These difficult verses are teaching the Colossians, and us, how to stand firm against false doctrines and corrupting spiritual influences. This is certainly needed in our confused generation when even people inside churches do not really know their Bibles. Paul links the significance of circumcision, the Old Testament 'sign of the covenant', with that of baptism in the New Testament. Each is a sign and symbol of God's activity, and the emphasis in baptism must always be first on what God has done in his act of saving us, rather than on our confession and response to that act. Baptism is spoken of as a death to sin and a resurrection to newness of life. The emphasis is on the fact that in Christ the 'old nature' is done away with; the dominion of sin has been broken; and all things have been made new, in the power of the resurrection. The illustration of being buried and raised emphasizes that this is not something we can do for ourselves. It is the activity of God.

The purpose of the illustration concerns the theology of salvation. The efficacy of baptism is not in its administration but in the death of Christ and the work of the Holy Spirit. Paul speaks of the working of God who raised Christ from the dead, and he seems to be urging the Colossian believers to recognize that this resurrection power is theirs in Christ (Eph. 1:15-21). In his commentary F. F. Bruce says, 'The putting off of the body of the flesh and its burial out of sight alike emphasized that the old life was a thing of the past.' That is why we need to forget the past. The break is complete. Everything is new in the risen life of Christ. This salvation is ours in Christ, to live by the indwelling power of the Holy Spirit. All the potential of the risen, victorious, life of Jesus Christ is ours. We are indeed complete in him.

Sovereign grace

Read also Ephesians 2:1-6,11-13

These verses are an elaboration of the exposition of salvation given in 1:12-14. Here, and in Ephesians 2:1-6,11-
13, Paul makes plain what it means *not* to be a believer and
this contrast causes salvation to be seen in glorious light.
Before we believed we were dead in sin, helpless and hopeless, in a state of total separation and alienation from God.
There was nothing we could do to help ourselves until we
were regenerated by the work of the Holy Spirit, and then,
hearing the gospel, we believed. Salvation is the work of
God's sovereign grace from beginning to end. God acted in
our state of disaster and inability, and he raised us *with*
Christ (as v. 12 shows). What he did *for* us he also accomplished *in* us to make the transformation complete.

In that great resurrection salvation God forgave all our
sins. They are dealt with, put away, and erased from the
record (Isa. 1:18; 38:17; 1 John 1:9). The totality and final-
ity of this forgiveness are spoken of in verse 14 in terms of
the signed acknowledgement of our bankruptcy and guilt
being taken away and nailed to the cross. Consider Pilate's
scrap of paper nailed to the cross, and compare it with our
Saviour going to God's Book (Rev. 20:12), and asking for
the page bearing your name, with all the detailed lifetime
record of every sin. He tears the page out of the book, carries
it to the cross, and cries in triumph, 'It is finished!' The
message from the cross declares for time and eternity that
all the sins, liabilities and guilt of the Christian have been
cancelled out. There is now nothing recorded against us in
the book. The law pronounced 'Guilty before God' and we
had no answer. The cross declares that for the believer there
is now no condemnation at all (Rom. 8:1). What a blessed
relief! What unspeakable joy and peace!

The devil defeated

Read also Revelation 12:7-12

Pray that we will never think of our salvation in a cheap or easy way. Sin was not overlooked or passed by. Its price was paid in full when the sinless Son of God died, the righteous for the unrighteous to bring us to God (1 Peter 3:18). But salvation is not just freedom from the guilt and power of sin (Rom. 6:14). We are told in verse 15 that our Lord Jesus Christ dealt with the accuser and blackmailer, breaking the power of the devil and all his accusing spirits. At times Satan focuses on our specific and obvious failures, but the Lord rebukes him (Zech. 3:1-5). The death of Jesus took away from the devil every ground he has ever had for pointing the finger at, and accusing and tormenting believers. Who can lay anything to the charge of God's elect, since it is God who declares them acquitted and justified in the face of every accusation (Rom. 8:33-34)?

We could link verse 15 with Paul's words in 2 Corinthians 2:14 where he speaks of our being led along in Christ's triumphal procession. Because he is the victor we are victors with him (1 Cor. 15:57). There will still be battles and struggle because we are still in the world and the devil never gives up (Luke 4:13; 1 Peter 5:8-9). We take our stand and resist on the basis of Christ's victory. The picture in Colossians is of the devil and all his satellite servants being led along in chains of defeat and humiliation in Christ's triumphant procession. We need to see clearly that the Bible teaches that the devil and his whole kingdom have been decisively defeated. There is no question of restoration for the devil. He may be angry, and very active, but he is finished (Rev. 12:12).

Rules and regulations

Read also Romans 14:1-13

In the matter of salvation Christ is everything. He is the way, and it is kept open by him for all who believe. He is the truth, and it is complete in him. He is the life, and it is given in fulness in him. Because this is so, Paul now urges the believers to guard their freedom. They must refuse to allow their lives to become controlled by rules, regulations, observances and prohibitions, which the false teachers insisted were necessary in order to go on with Christ and to grow spiritually. We need to guard against any form of legalism. We can *choose* to deny ourselves on various levels, to deny ourselves various pleasures, and to accept a way of life that is narrower than it needs to be. But it must be done freely by our own volition and for love of Jesus Christ, and not because it is a requirement imposed upon us by individuals or organizations. We must also guard against any forms of 'ritual', taking that word in its widest sense. Conforming to 'patterns' of spiritual life can so easily take our minds and hearts away from Christ, with the result that we become pleased with our own spirituality and too concerned about whether or not people approve of us and consider us mature.

We must also be careful before we pronounce on other people's activities if they do not conform to what we regard as a 'right' way of life for an evangelical believer. Consider what Paul says in Romans 14:1-13. Think of how Jesus opposed the legalism of the Pharisees in Mark 7:1-8,14-19. True spiritual life is walking in fellowship with God, and not the keeping of arbitrary rules, even when the rules have an appearance of spirituality and biblical truth.

Freedom in Christ

Read also 1 Corinthians 10:23-33

When rules, routines, observances and prohibitions become the focus, Christian life becomes hard, legalistic, unattractive and graceless. Paul, by the Holy Spirit, insists that we must refuse to give in to those who would impose such restrictions and requirements upon us. This does not lead to indulgence, because if we are truly Christ's then we will want above all else to live to please him. If we are walking with Christ then we will learn from him to have a care for others. We will live life in such a way that we will not hinder or confuse other Christians who may not be so sure of their liberty in Christ as we are. Read 1 Corinthians 8:7-13; 10:23-33. Paul knew that the false teachers troubling the Colossians were intense legalists, very aware of the requirements and prohibitions of the Old Testament. But in Christ we are no longer under obligation to the Law.

Although the Law pointed forward to Christ, foreshadowing the truth he was to reveal and the salvation he was to accomplish, now that Christ has come we live in the full light of his presence and his finished work. There is no longer shadow. We walk in the full light of God. We live under a new regime, one which no longer terrorizes us nor seeks to control us by fear of judgement. We live now by the law of love, which on the one hand inspires us to respond in eager service to please him who first loved us, and on the other hand restrains us and holds us back from self-will and self-indulgence (2 Cor. 5:14-15). Just as the Lord Jesus delighted to do the will of the Father (Ps. 40:7-8, AV), so must we. We do not live by detailed laws, but by the law of love (Matt. 22:34-40). How sad it is to see believers hemmed in by fear of what people will say if they break one of the 'rules' made by tradition.

Pride

Read also Matthew 23:1-12

Whoever the false teacher or teachers were, they must have been amazed by the directness and intensity of Paul's strictures. They were promising 'deeper' spirituality but Paul charged them with disqualifying the Christians, turning them away from Christ, robbing them of their rights and blessing. It seems that some claimed to have had an extraordinary experience of God or a vision not granted to others. Of course, when such a subjective, private experience is claimed no one is really in a position to say it has not happened. The person concerned becomes, in his own eyes and, alas, in the eyes of others, a 'special' minister or teacher.

Paul seems to have a particular individual in mind, as verse 18 indicates. He describes him as puffed up, swollen in head and heart, sensuous, self-gratifying, self-centred and adrift from Christ since he does not hold to the Head. He is a law to himself. He is proud of his spirituality, not realizing that that is a complete contradiction of spirituality. It seems almost as if Paul is questioning whether the man is a Christian at all. He does not take his place or play his part in the body, which is the church. He seems to believe that he has no need of any spiritual help or encouragement or nourishment from other believers because he is so totally self-sufficient. He is the kind of man who loves to teach but not to listen. He is continually seeking some avenue by which he can express his 'gifts' which, he is quite sure, will be admired by all who see them. This kind of man has his horizon filled with himself. Christ just does not come into it. And those who are taken in by him will live to regret the day that they listened to him rather than to those faithful men who had first shown them Christ in all his pre-eminence and full sufficiency.

True humility

Read also 2 Corinthians 12:1-10

We need to consider this false spirituality so that we will be better able to discern and refute false teachers and their baneful influence. Paul had an amazing experience but kept totally quiet about it for years, speaking of it only in order to counter the spiritual pride of others (2 Cor. 12:1-10). False humility is an unattractive performance that can be switched on for the occasion. It is not real and it is *self-*conscious. Angel worship is difficult to define. It may refer to initiation rites; or heavenly beings called in to help experiences; or intermediaries of a non-human kind, copying the angels of Jacob's dream in Genesis 28:10-17; or even some occult or cultic creatures with an aura of the 'heavenly' about them. But regarding these in any way as mediators in dealing with God is totally heretical since it displaces the one Mediator (1 Tim. 2:5).

We have already spoken of visions, and any vision that does not cause us to fall down in utter humility before God, convicting us of our sin and unworthiness, is simply not from God. Consider both Isaiah (Isa. 6:1-5) and John (Rev. 1:12-18). Paul says that the particular man in Colosse has no reason whatever to think he is spiritual. Everything about him declares that beneath his facade of spirituality lies an uncrucified heart. The final evidence is that he is a detached or disembodied member, not a real part of the body. Such people never find a congregation spiritual enough to settle in. They are looking for a place where they will be recognized and admired by all. Such people could never make the claim Paul makes in 2 Corinthians 4:5,7. What comfort and security there is in being an ordinary member, a part of the body along with others! Such a life is anything but ordinary (1 Cor. 12:14-26, especially v. 22).

Real holiness

Read also Psalm 16:1-11

Paul now issues a challenge to the Christians, seeking to jolt them into an awareness of how they have allowed themselves to be duped by false teachers and led away from true faith in, and commitment to, Christ. The 'basic principles' of this world (v. 20) can be understood in two ways. The phrase can refer to the worldly idea that we are saved by good works, by our own efforts, so that we really play a part in our own salvation. But there is also a suggestion here of a satanic influence. It is the devil who aims to distract from the glory of Christ and to draw away disciples into an inferior way of Christian life under the guise of leading them on to higher things.

The devil can appear very spiritual at times (2 Cor. 11:14). But if we understand that in Christ we have been delivered not only from sin but also from the powers of evil, then we will be aware that the elements, or the essentials, of this wicked world have no part in our living for God. We no longer belong to this world and we must not allow ourselves to be pressurized and conditioned by it (Rom. 12:1-2). Nor must we allow anyone to narrow down and inhibit our glorious life and liberty in Christ by a tyranny of rules and regulations which have their origin in mere men and not in God. There is a 'holiness', a 'separation from the world', that is essentially legalistic, but which serves no purpose in the basic business of 'dying to self'. We are to be in the world but not of it, using it but not abusing it (1 Cor. 7:31). It is when we look to Christ and live in Christ that we move away from sin and into true holiness of life. It is then that we discover the fulness of life that Jesus spoke of in John 10:10. There *are* harmless pleasures, and God gives us all things richly to enjoy (1 Tim. 6:17).

Royal family

Read also 1 John 3:1-3

Paul has given a glorious exposition of the salvation we have in Christ and now begins a comprehensive application to the practicalities of living as Christians in a godless society. These verses should inspire us to want to be all that we are meant to be. They declare the principles and attitudes that enable us to be so. It is in looking to Christ that we become quietly and peacefully aware of what we should allow in our lives and what we should keep away from. But it is not all challenge; it is also encouragement.

We must always remember we have a God who knows our frailties and limitations (Ps. 103:13-14). He is the God who does not snuff out the feeble flame of devotion nor does he break the weak, struggling life of discipleship (Isa. 42:3). Our God is not in the business of demolition and discouragement but the very opposite. Paul takes us to the facts. *Since* we have died with Christ to sin, self and Satan; *since* we have been raised with Christ to newness of life; *since* we have a great and glorious Saviour seated at God's right hand; *since* we have in him an inheritance, incorruptible, undefiled that never fades; *since* this is our true identity, status and destiny; and *since* we have an unspeakably glorious future in this world and the next, is it not time that we began to live as if we realized all this was true? Consider how poised those who are of royal blood appear. They know they are royal and it is natural for them to be true to what they are. In Christ we too are of royal blood; we belong to the family of the King of kings. We should remember this and live accordingly. Read Ephesians 1:3-6; 2:4-7; 1 Peter 2:9; and 1 John 3:1-3.

Grasp the truth

Read also 2 Corinthians 4:16-18

We must be true to what God has made us in Christ and let it be seen in the way we live. There are deliberate decisions and choices to be made in the areas of attitude and ambition. We can think of this in a similar way to marriage. When the vows are taken and the declaration made that we are married, then we must believe the fact, live the part and be true to our new status. We must resist all temptation to go back and live as if we had not been married. That would be a contradiction and would lead to confusion, hurt and shame.

So it is with us who are united to Christ. We must see things from the perspective of eternity and, recognizing that in a very real sense we have been severed from this present wicked world, we should seek the things that are above. This is a practical and deliberate attitude, as Paul showed in his own costly life (2 Cor. 4:16-18). It was this 'seeing him who is invisible' that enabled Moses to endure, and to evaluate faithfulness to God and his people more highly than everything else (Heb. 11:24-27).

Paul is specific about what we should focus on. It is Christ, seated at the right hand of God, his work finished and the issues of life no longer in doubt (Heb. 1:3; Phil. 2:9-11; 1 Cor. 15:25). We must also think of Christ at the right hand of the Father in glory as the one who 'pleads our cause at God's right hand, omnipotent to save'.[9] Read Romans 8:34 and Hebrews 7:25. It is good to refer again and again to such verses so that the truth will be imprinted in our minds and hearts. If we do not know our position, our possessions and our potential in Christ, we will never rise to true Christian living.

Set free to live

Read also John 8:31-36

The emphasis in verse 2 is on our minds not our emotions. This is important because our feelings are neither constant nor dependable. The facts are that the salvation we have in Christ has involved us in a death and resurrection like his (Rom. 6:5). The life we have is hid with total security with Christ in God. The things that matter and have abiding value are the things of eternity, not the temporary things of this world. The things of earth cannot ever finally frustrate God's purposes for us and this gives us encouragement to go on when life is really difficult. We set our minds on 'things above'. This does not mean we go about with a faraway, ethereal look on our faces, being 'so heavenly minded that we are no earthly use'. But it does mean that, living in the power of the world to come (Heb. 6:5, AV), we refuse to allow this world, with its past, present or future influences and pressures, to dominate and control our lives. Our lives are for Christ, and we have been set free to live them.

Of course, all sorts of mental, emotional and cultural influences may have operated on our personalities in our earlier lives. Christ can lead us out of any inherited legacy of emotional complication. Some may have been neglected and manipulated in childhood, adolescence and even adulthood, and were driven in on themselves. Some had evil things done to them, leaving scars which have distorted and inhibited personality. The devil seeks to use all these things to keep us in bondage and hold us back. Christ can open all these prison cells and set us free to be our real selves in him. But it calls for a conscious acceptance of the facts of salvation and an instructed discipline of thought. If Christ has made us new, set us free and lives within us by the Holy Spirit, the possibilities are limitless.

Christ is coming

Read also 2 Timothy 4:6-9

We must still consider verse 4, which reminds us of the fact that at some specific point in history Christ will return in glory. This is something we tend to forget. It is not often preached, but it is clear in Scripture (Acts 1:9-11; 1 Thess. 4:13-18; Matt. 24:42-44). We need to be ready. The particular emphasis in verse 4 is that we shall stand before Christ in glory. Then he shall see of the travail of his soul, the fruit of his suffering, and will be satisfied (Isa. 53:11, AV). It is not yet known what we shall be, but we shall be like him, and that will indeed be wonderful (1 John 3:1-3). We need the reassurance that God is able to keep us from falling and to present us faultless in his presence with exceeding joy, for him and also for us (Jude 24).

We must learn to think of our destiny in Christ. Consider Philippians 3:20 - 4:1 and then read what Jesus says in John 17:22-26. It is little wonder that John urges us to live so that we will not be ashamed before him at his coming (1 John 2:28). Here in Colossians Paul is not exhorting but stating what will be when Christ comes. It will be manifest that, in Christ, from the moment of our conversion (and indeed long before that in the purposes of God) we were destined for glory. We were marked out to take our place with Christ in his glory. All the promises given in Christ will have reached their fulfilment and perfection. Think of such verses as 2 Corinthians 3:18 and realize that we are in fact being prepared for that glory. The assurances of the gospel thrill our hearts and constrain us to worship. We begin to have a fresh understanding of the great words of Wesley's hymn, which encourages us to cast our crowns before him, lost in wonder, love and praise.[10]

The fight of faith

Read also Romans 6:17-23

In the fight of faith we must use our minds and grasp ever more clearly the facts of our salvation. The potential we have in Christ and the possibilities for life and service are greater than anything we can imagine or pray for (Eph. 3:20). From the story of Nicodemus (John 3:1-8) we must grasp the thought of being 'born again', being made new creatures in Christ, possessed of a new life within us by the power of the indwelling Holy Spirit. The possibilities of the different kind of life open to us are indeed limitless. But possibilities have to be realized and that calls not only for faith but also for the effort of faith.

Christian believers live on two planes. We are united to Christ and belong to the world to come but we still live in this world. We are new people in Christ but we are still 'in the body', and our 'old nature' has still to be dealt with. But it is not an evenly balanced struggle, because the victory of Christ is now within us and can be counted on. Be clear about this. The believer does not struggle *towards* victory. We start on victory ground in Christ and, asserting that victory, we are called to deal decisively with everything in our personality and life that is contrary to Christ. There is a clear link here with what Paul says in Romans 6:19 about yielding our bodies, our capacities, our potential and inclinations, to the purpose of God in righteousness and holiness. If Christians gave themselves over to a life of holiness and Christian service with the enthusiasm they once gave to pleasure and sin, the world might once again be shaken (Acts 17:6, AV).

War against sin

Read also Romans 7:15-25

There is nothing superficial about the challenge of Paul's words. He calls for nothing less than a death to every aspect and disposition of sin (Rom. 6:11). It requires a determined and settled attitude of refusal in respect of all that is contrary to God. If God cannot bless it, we have no right to have it.

The need for such a radical attitude is threefold. Firstly, there is the legacy of our past life which leaves a vulnerability mentally, emotionally and psychologically. Secondly, there is the atmosphere of fallen society with its seductive influence, always enticing us to return to the life we once knew, and which kindles into awareness at times with little warning. And thirdly, there is the reality of our old, fallen nature and the conflict with our new nature in Christ which Paul speaks of so vividly in Romans 7:15-25; 8:5-13. The life of faith is essentially the fight of faith: the fight to believe what we are and have in Christ, and to claim the victory in every area of life and experience. In seeking to stand in gospel victory a believer can become demoralized because of many failures. But we must not be distracted. We must claim the promised forgiveness and the ongoing cleansing by the blood of Jesus Christ (1 John 1:7-9), and go on to affirm that we stand in Christ's complete victory. As we wage war on the things that belong to the past, remember that there is a devil who constantly stirs these alien feelings and desires in us with the clear objective of stealing our peace, spoiling our fellowship with God and hindering our service. When once we see what sin can steal from us and from those we are bound up with, we will be much more radical in our attitude to it. We need the determination expressed in Micah 7:8.

Sin is dangerous

Read also James 4:1-7

The list of sins given here and amplified in verses 8-9 gives
some indication of the kind of life from which these Christians had been rescued, and we should rejoice that we have
a Saviour who is able to save to the uttermost (Heb. 7:25,
AV). If, by the grace of God, we have been kept from things
that are repulsive and ugly we should be thankful to God,
and to those whose influence contributed to our protection.
But we must never be complacent, not even if we have
been Christians a long time and feel that we are past such
dangers. Many a person has said sadly, 'I never thought
that would happen to me.' There is a devil and sin still has
the fascination it had in the Garden of Eden. We need to
watch and pray lest we fall into temptation (Matt. 26:41)
and this is why we need the *whole* armour of God (Eph.
6:10-18).

We must learn where we are specially vulnerable, keep
out of the way of sin, and deal with its enticements the
moment they begin. We must not trifle. The atmosphere of
our generation is sordid and infectious, and this is one
reason why we need to share regularly in worship so that
the fresh air of God's truth will clean, revive and strengthen
us. The Bible is honest and practical, and the first two sins
in the list refer to sexual immorality and perversion. Paul
goes on to speak of passion or sensual craving in the area of
physical sensation, and then evil desire, desire for what is
forbidden, perhaps simply because it is forbidden. The list
here ends with covetousness, which is described as idolatry.
The coveting may be related particularly to the area of sexual
sin because it craves for what belongs to another. The whole
list seems to be summed up in idolatry. I, my, me and mine
become the whole of life. It displaces God.

Clean lives

Read also Ephesians 4:17-24

To see ever more clearly the glory of salvation and the power of God to 'rescue the perishing' read 1 Corinthians 6:9-11; Ephesians 4:17-24; 5:3-11; Galatians 5:16-21; and the terrible description of fallen society in Romans 1:18-32. In the face of such flagrant human sin it is not surprising that God's wrath is declared and is in fact operating in the world. This is what we have been saved out of, and it is as we go on with Christ that we begin to see the exceeding ugliness, offensiveness and power of sin. We become aware of how much we owe to the sovereign grace of God that sought us, found us, lifted us up, and brought us out of darkness into light, from the power of Satan to God (Acts 26:18). Little wonder Paul tells us to put all these evil things away. Not only do they give us nothing (Rom. 6:20-21), but by their lies they also rob us of what God promises us. Sin is a lie. It does not lead to fulfilment as the tempter suggested (Gen. 3:1-7), but when it has worked all its evil destructive work in our lives it brings death (James 1:13-15). We must put all these things away, as we would cast away filthy cloths, because we neither need them nor want them.

The sins mentioned in verse 8 can come easily to all of us. Anger is an attitude of enmity that bears a grudge. The poet Robert Burns speaks of someone 'nursing her wrath to keep it warm'.[11] Rage is the outburst of bad temper. Malice and slander are ill-will and ill-speaking. This is gossip that hurts and causes trouble, even when the speaker protests no harm was intended. The word for slander is literally blasphemy, which denigrates and devalues the person spoken of. Filthy language is anything that has an open or underlying suggestion of impurity. If we realized we were in Jesus' company we would not trifle with any of these things.

No distinctions

Read also Romans 3:21-30

Paul is speaking about Christian behaviour in the church, and if we cannot live Christlike lives among believers, it is most unlikely that we will live right lives in the world. The previous note reminded us that we walk in Jesus' company all the time. We are his people, and that is why we must deal with each other as Christ has dealt with us. This should be our natural desire now because we have put off the old nature and put on the new nature which, by the activity of the Holy Spirit within us, is being progressively transformed into the likeness of Jesus. If we give way to any of the sins spoken of in verses 8-9 there should be an instant feeling of shame and unhappiness because the Spirit of God within us will be grieved. We should also feel guilty because we will have grieved others and caused ripples of unrest within the fellowship of those who are together with him just as we are. It is this disturbance to fellowship which is the theme of today's single verse.

The tensions and oppositions which are accepted as normal and inevitable (and even desirable by some) in un-regenerate society are simply not allowed in the fellowship of believers (Gal. 3:28; Eph. 4:3). Differences of background, tradition, liturgy, education, culture, social status or anything else are not allowed to make distinctions in the church. Christ is everything and each of us owes everything to him (1 Cor. 4:7). In that context we owe everything to each other. Note clearly that Paul does not suggest that doctrinal differences are unimportant, nor does he in any way comment here on the distinction of function between men and women in the church. But keep in mind that when Christ is everything then, and only then, is there harmony.

The old and the new

Read also Luke 18:9-14

At this point it is helpful to look at the structure of this section of the epistle. In 3:5-11 the theme is 'Get rid of'. In 3:12-17 it is 'Put on'. In 3:18 - 4:1 it is 'obedience'. In 4:2-6 it is 'Watch and pray'. Getting rid of something is fruitless, and can even be dangerous, unless there is a corresponding act of 'putting on', as we are reminded by Jesus' story in Luke 11:24-26. An empty heart, an empty mind and an empty life are an invitation to the devil. A personality that is simply negative, devoid of obvious vices, may be correct but it can lead to pride and is cold and unattractive (Luke 18:9-14). We need to reflect the warmth of true humanity as it is in the Jesus who lives in our hearts and wants to be seen in our lives. In Romans 13:14 Paul describes this as 'clothing' ourselves with the Lord Jesus Christ, making no provision or *wrong* allowances for the flesh. We emphasize the word 'wrong' because there is a denying and a neglect of the human aspects of our lives that is simply not Christian, as Paul has already made plain in 2:20-23. Some self-denial is in fact self-indulgence because its object and effect is to draw attention to ourselves.

Verse 12 lists five graces that should mark our lives, and each of them should cause us to think of Jesus. Together in a human life they constitute a great attraction. It was when people saw these graces in Jesus' life and sensed them when he spoke that they drew near to him. We may have sung, 'Let the beauty of Jesus be seen in me, all his wondrous compassion and purity'.[12] That is a prayer that God longs to answer. But it will mean a big change in our lives as, with strong determination day after day, we resolutely put off the old and put on the new.

Real kindness

Read also Luke 7:36-47

These verses speak of those whom God has chosen to be the 'windows' in which he can display to the world his marvellous grace (Eph. 1:4; 2:7). We are hand-picked, chosen and lifted out of brokenness and darkness by God's own hand, through his Son, our Saviour. Because we are 'in Christ' we are holy, clothed in righteousness divine. Our life-stream partakes of his holiness: it is eternal life. We are dearly loved by God, the objects and recipients of his endless love which defies measurement (Eph. 3:18-19). Because we have received love in such measure it is our spiritual duty to show the same love to others (1 John 4:11). There is no reason why we should hesitate. If we dare to talk about whether or not people deserve our love, then *we* have forgotten the teaching of Jesus in Matthew 18:21-35 and Luke 7:36-47.

In Paul's list of graces the first two, compassion and kindness, are in relation to others. These words speak of a heart of care that expresses itself in word and action. But love is not sentimental weakness because true care always has as its objective the good of the one being ministered to. That means, as parents well know, that sometimes the most plaintive and insistent requests have to be denied, even when the requests become demands, backed up with threats of blackmail. It is in this area that we begin to see just how costly love can be. At the same time it is sensitive, becoming aware of the person's need before they themselves are, and beginning to minister without waiting for the person to ask for help. It is not a Christlike attitude to say, 'If he/she had asked I would have been glad to help. They only had to ask.' Usually it is after Jesus has drawn near to us that we begin to ask from him. Being a Christian is a very practical thing.

Patience

Read also Matthew 5:1-10,43-48

The next two graces in verses 12, humility and gentleness, should be significant marks of our personalities. Why should it ever be otherwise? What are we apart from the grace of God? The only things we can really claim as our own doing are our sins, and they are nothing to be proud of. It is God alone who has enabled us to be persons of worth and, in his gracious dealings with us, he has used other people to whom we must ever be grateful, not least for their prayers. Isn't it strange how seldom we thank people for praying for us, for encouraging us, and for showing us an example of how to live and serve as Christians? We owe so much to other people, and to recognize this is a corrective to pride. How we need to come to grips with the exhortation, 'Let this mind be in you, which was also in Christ Jesus,' (Phil. 2:5, AV). We need to follow his example of gracious submission and uncomplaining trust (Phil. 2:1-8; 1 Peter 2:21-23).

The next three graces (vv. 12-13), patience, forbearance and a forgiving spirit, take us again into the area of relationships with others, especially with regard to our reactions to what they say and do. It takes real patience not to react in haste and anger, and we must learn to be long-suffering just as God has been with us. Instead of becoming tired of people and their complications, we must learn to bear with one another. It helps if we try to discern why people are so brittle, spiky, on edge and demanding. Sometimes it is simply because they are finding life, and themselves, hard to cope with. Thinking like this is far better and far more helpful than just dismissing people because we feel they are complicated, inadequate and too much of a problem.

The fruit of the Spirit

Read also 1 Corinthians 13:1-13

In the context of Paul's words about forgiving and loving one another the word for forgiving is basically the word 'grace' (*charis* in the Greek), from which we have our word 'charismatic'. Paul, therefore, is describing the charismatic Christian, not in terms of the more demonstrative 'gifts', but rather in terms of the fruit of the Spirit: those graces which the Lord longs to see manifested in the life of every believer (Gal. 5:22-26). Whatever gifts we have, or think we have, whether they are intellectual, social, cultural or spiritual, if they do not progressively make us like Jesus then they have little real worth.

Paul does not discuss who is right or wrong in the matter of the specific grievances he seems to refer to. That is secondary. First and foremost, there should be forgiveness and, if that is sought from the heart right away, then, when the two parties come together to air their differences, there will be hope from the start. It is not easy to forgive when someone has wounded your feelings deeply or hurt someone we love. That is why we must not react. We must let the initial hurt settle, our anger cool, our attitude and intention be brought into the presence of the Jesus who has forgiven us so often. Only then are we ready to go and speak. Of course, 'Love is always eager to believe the best'[13] and it may indicate how little we know about love that we so often start by thinking the worst. The devil will gladly push us along that road, magnifying and intensifying all we feel about the hurt. That will make us see the other person in the worst possible light. How we need to pray, 'Forgive us our debts as we forgive our debtors.' Remember also the startling words at the end of the Lord's Prayer, recorded in Matthew 6:14-15.

The peace of Christ

Read also Mark 4:35-41

This verse is absolute in its exhortation. It makes us think
of the Prince of Peace, who commanded the wind and waves
to cease and brought peace to the frightened disciples on
the Sea of Galilee (Mark 4:35-41). Let the peace of Christ,
the peace he has made through his cross, the peace of his
presence, rule in your hearts. 'Let every inward debate between self and God, between self and others, be ruled and
guided by the deep consciousness that in Christ you are
indeed at rest; let the plea for self-assertion be ever met
and negatived by the decision of that umpire in favour of
love.'[14] The picture is of Christ acting as the chairman of
the meeting when all the affairs of life are being discussed.
Any stirring of conflict, criticism or disruption is immediately called to order and peace is re-established. Remember the words of Isaiah 59:19: 'When the enemy shall come
in like a flood, the Spirit of the LORD shall lift up a standard
against him' (AV). This is what God always wants to do for
us, because he is the God of peace (Heb. 13:20). Come to
him constantly in prayer, with thanksgiving, so that his
peace will stand guard over our hearts and minds (Phil.
4:4-7). As soon as our thoughts begin to race (usually head-
ing for confusion) the word is simple, 'Be still, and know
that I am God' (Ps. 46:10).

Consider the picture in Psalm 23 of the Lord preparing a
table of rest and refreshing in the presence of the enemy.
Without forgetting the reality of the spiritual battle, we can
let peace rule in our hearts. After all, Jesus commanded us
not to let our hearts be troubled, but to trust him, who gives
us his own peace (John 14:1,27). Wherever we are, if we
say to ourselves, 'Jesus is here; he is in charge,' we will
begin to know his peace. We will be thankful.

Peace, perfect peace

Read also Hebrews 13:20-21

There is hunger for peace in our restless, frightening world and Jesus is the kind of person whose presence, even without a word being spoken, brings that peace.

All kinds of agitation are subdued by him. The Christmas message speaks of peace (Luke 2:14). The message of the cross speaks of peace (Col. 1:20). The resurrection story speaks of peace (John 20:19-21). Remember the promise in Isaiah 26:3 and the prayer in 2 Thessalonians 3:16. Many of the epistles begin with reference to peace from the Father and the Son. Peace of mind, heart and spirit is a wonderful blessing, and gospel peace is based on facts. Consider the following words of this hymn by E. H. Bickersteth, some of which we have noted before:

Peace, perfect peace, in this dark world of sin?
The blood of Jesus whispers peace within.

Peace, perfect peace, by thronging duties pressed?
To do the will of Jesus, this is rest.

Peace, perfect peace with loved ones far away?
In Jesus' keeping we are safe, and they.

Peace, perfect peace, our future all unknown?
Jesus we know, and He is on the throne.

Peace, perfect peace, death shadowing us and ours?
Jesus has vanquished death and all its powers.

The only gospel

Read also Galatians 1:6-9

Here is another magnificent single verse full of profound and practical spiritual counsel. Verse 15 spoke of the body, the fellowship of believers which is the church, and called for thankfulness. The verse before that (v. 14) called for harmony within the fellowship. Now we are shown that in such a context the word of Christ will have full freedom to operate both in individual lives and in and through the church in ministry.

The 'word of Christ' is the word about Christ and the word proceeding from Christ. The ministry of the church is not an area for speculation and philosophy. The message is a 'given' message (Gal. 1:11-12), a complete and exclusive message, for Christ himself declared that he was the way, the truth and the life: the only way to the Father (John 14:6). The apostles said the same, declaring that there was only one name whereby people can be saved (Acts 4:12). The Old Testament Scriptures affirmed the same message, as the risen Christ made plain on the road to Emmaus (Luke 24:25-27). The word of Christ has to do with the message of the faith given by God once for all (Jude 3), and there is no other gospel to preach (Gal. 1:6-9). Without doubt Paul is seeking to ground the believers in a love for and trust in the Scriptures, which alone are able to make us wise unto salvation because they are God-given and God-breathed (2 Tim. 3:14-17). There is much more to say and to learn about the 'word of Christ', but note how the theme of thankfulness occurs in three successive verses (vv. 15-17). When so many are without the Word at all, many without real ministry, and others with little or no fellowship, we must make sure we never take our gospel privileges for granted.

Study the Word

Read also Hebrews 2:1-3; 4:1-2

Most people know, love and rejoice in John 3:16 and we do well to commit to memory this '3:16', along with others such as 2 Timothy 3:16; Malachi 3:16; Daniel 3:16-18; and 1 Corinthians 3:16. The importance of the Word of Christ, the Word of God (John 1:1-4,14), cannot be overemphasized in the life of the believer and the church. All our thinking must be instructed, guided and corrected by the Word of God, otherwise we will live our lives not just according to our own ideas but influenced largely by our feelings. Our attitudes become conditioned by sentiment rather than truth. When troubles threaten us, instead of considering them in the light of God's truth as shown in such passages as James 1:2-4; 1 Peter 4:12-14; and Romans 5:3-5, we can react emotionally and the peace Jesus said was our rightful inheritance is snatched away from us.

We need to receive, know and respond to God's Word all the time, especially when we are accustomed to regular preaching of the Word, lest familiarity leads to carelessness (Heb. 2:1; 4:1-2). We must come to grips with Scripture, not just in its simplicity but in its strength and difficulty so that we will grow up into spiritual maturity (1 Peter 2:2; Heb. 5:11-14). In order to meet effectively the temptations of the devil we must be well grounded in our understanding of Scripture. In the story of our Lord's temptation in Matthew 4:4-11 it was by standing on the truth and promises of Scripture that the victory was won. In the account of the resurrection in Luke 24:44-49 it was on the basis of their understanding of Scripture that the disciples were able to grasp the significance of spiritual events and so were prepared for future service.

Taught by the Word

Read also Psalm 119:9-16

We begin to understand why the psalmist loves God's law and makes it his meditation to be pondered over throughout the day (Ps. 119:97). It not only feeds and builds us up, it is a Word that permeates even to the unconscious mind, exercises moral influence and leads us in holy dedication into the service of God (Ps. 119:9; Eph. 5:26; John 17:17). By this same Word we are built up and integrated into the everlasting purposes of God (Acts 20:32). But we must see clearly that in this verse Paul is speaking of the influence and effect of the Word of Christ in relation to the life of the congregation and fellowship.

The first point he makes concerns our responsibility in terms of instruction and correction of each other. But this must be done with wisdom, grace and understanding, as well as in truth; with careful tact and not with blundering insensitivity. At times truth must be held back because people are neither ready nor able to receive it (John 16:12). Words spoken at the wrong time, however well-meaning we may be, can have the opposite effect from what we intended. In Psalm 106:32-33 there is a serious lesson to be learned regarding the way we speak to one another. We are reminded that the wrong-spirited words of the congregation put such pressure on Moses that he spoke rashly and unadvisedly to the people, with significant after-effects on himself (Num. 20:2-13). How we need to let our hearts be subdued by the Word so that our lips will not cause damage to others and to the work of God (James 3:3-10)! We still have the final part of the verse to deal with but we have enough to think and pray about for one day.

Praise is for God

Read also 1 Chronicles 16:7-14,23-29

The Word of Scripture in its full authority must be the inspiration and control the content of all we mean by Christian praise. It is to God that our praises are directed and the important thing is that he should be honoured rather than that we should enjoy the singing. This means the praise items used in a service are an integral part of all we mean by worship. Praise should never be an off-the-cuff, 'happy-clappy' sing-song during which people are not really thinking about the words. There should be glorious biblical truth in what we sing, so that we are drawn together and learn together as we sing. In this way our praises are an expression of worship, gratitude, thanksgiving and dedication.

When praise is sung with hearts kindled with gratitude to God there is a glorious congregational witness to the fact that we have a God who deserves the highest praise. This is why the words and the music of Christian praise should be worthy, with theological and devotional substance, *and* have some degree of continuity and permanence. Hymns and choruses that are weak and repetitive (and which fall out of use and are forgotten like fashions that change) have little to contribute to true worship. This is important in the area of what we teach children to sing. If they are never introduced to the great hymns of the faith and the life of the church while they are young, they will be seriously deprived in later years when their understanding has developed. There is no need to make strict identification of the different items of praise mentioned. But our final emphasis must be that praise is directed towards God and it is for him and his pleasure. God is enthroned on (or inhabits, AV) the praises of his people (Ps. 22).

Witness by life

Read also Matthew 5:13-16

There is something gloriously comprehensive here. Whatever we do, in word or deed, in the church or wherever we
go, we are to do it in the name of and for the glory of the
Lord Jesus Christ, giving thanks to the Father through him
for such a wonderful Saviour. There is profound and clear
guidance here regarding all manner of activities. Can we
do them in the name of Jesus and can we thank God for the
opportunity to do these things? Whatever we are doing we
need to remember that we bear the name of Jesus and are
marked out in society as his people. We confess him as
Lord with our lips, and our whole way of life, including
our attitudes, must bear out and confirm that confession.

We must remember Jesus said that not all who call him
Lord are his disciples, but only those who do his will (Matt.
7:21-23). Whatever privileges and liberties we allow ourselves in Christian life or whatever restrictions we place
on ourselves and our activities, all must be guided by and
accomplished for the glory of God (1 Cor. 10:31). This way
of life is not followed out of a sense of duty, or to conform
to a set of rules imposed by the tradition of any Christian
organization or by some powerful personality. It is a way of
life motivated by love to the Lord Jesus, a glad yielding to
his will with a spirit of thanksgiving. This contrasts radi-
cally with the spirit of discontent in our pleasure-seeking
society with its demands for 'rights', and even with the
grudging spirit of service found so often in the life of congregations. Of course, if we always ask ourselves, 'What is
the Christian thing to do?' we must see to it that our thinking is instructed rightly and moulded by God's truth. That
is the way to know his will (Rom. 12:1-2).

Witness at home

Read also Matthew 19:3-6

We take these two verses together because husband and wife are one flesh and what God has joined together must not be divided (Matt. 19:3-6). In verses 12-17 we were counselled to be Christlike and God-glorifying in every part of the life of the church. But we must be the same in our home life, else our Christianity is a mockery. If the standard is living for the Lord in sweet and glad obedience in the church, then it must be the same in home and family relationships, so that in everything God is glorified and pleased.

The place where our sanctification is put to the test is not in church meetings and services where we are being officially holy, but in the daily routine of home and family life. At breakfast in the rush to get children to school and ourselves to work in time; in the evening when all are tired and apt to be irritable; at meal times when the telephone interrupts; these are the times when we have to be Christlike. What point is there in being affable in dealing with people, showing interest and care at church if at home we lapse into silent selfishness, making no effort to help, to listen or to encourage? What point is there in having a *reputation* for being spiritual if at home we only speak of God to justify bossiness? Yes, Christians can be like that. The people at church do not see this. But God sees. So do the others in the family. A Christian marriage is much more than just two Christians being married; and a Christian home is much more than just a number of related Christians living together. Relationships and attitudes have to be Christian and the whole of life has to be in accord with the pattern, purpose and will of God as it is made plain in Scripture. Ephesians 5:25-33 is a searching passage from which we cannot escape.

God's pattern

Read also Ephesians 5:21-23

The important words 'in the Lord' signify that all human relationships are linked with and governed by our relationship to Christ. *No one* has the right to lord it over another because we are *all* under the lordship of Christ. The important thing is that all relationships should conform to the pattern of the will of God, and Paul has in mind the original order of creation and the 'headship' of man. There is no suggestion that the woman is humanly or spiritually inferior to or less important than the man.

That this was Paul's personal and practical attitude is seen in his warm comments and thanksgiving for those women who were his fellow-labourers in the gospel (Phil. 4:3; Rom. 16:1-3). He would also have known of the actions of Mary Magdalene at the resurrection and women such as Deborah in the book of Judges. But these individual cases have nothing to do with the question of women serving as elders or ministers in the church, nor indeed in the question of relationships between the sexes. This is not the place to discuss all the issues so passionately argued by 'feminists' today. Much has been written about such themes, often qualifying the Scriptures by insisting that they are bounded by time and conditioned by culture. That is simply saying that the Scriptures are not God's clear Word to this and every generation. Once we adopt that attitude the door is open to qualifying and denying the authority of the Word of God in all issues of faith and life. There is no suggestion that the woman's opinion does not matter but there is every suggestion that it is God's pattern that matters. That pattern leads to fulness of life, dignity, satisfaction and service. Submission to God's will and glad acceptance of God's pattern is the standard for men and women.

Relationships and prayer

Read also 1 Peter 3:1-7

In some marriages only one partner is a Christian believer. This was often the situation in apostolic times and the Bible addresses the issue. God's pattern for behaviour still holds good. In 1 Peter 3:7 note the phrase, 'heirs together of the grace of life' (AV). Peter makes it plain that right relationships between husband and wife are necessary if their prayer life is not to be hindered. If we read Proverbs 31:10-12,27-28 we begin to see how a husband needs the 'help-meet', the encourager and enabler, in order that he might become all that God desires him to be. But the husband must be a true Christian husband, loving his wife with the highest kind of human and spiritual love, which requires him, as a spiritual duty, to give to his wife the unceasing care and the sacrificial, self-denying love that is hers by right. It is the kind of love that Christ showed to the church when he gave himself up for her (Eph. 5:25). The husband's priority is the well-being of his wife, not his own comfort and satisfaction.

When Paul commands husbands not to be harsh, he is thinking not only of petty tyranny but also of how easy it is for a husband simply to neglect his wife, taking her for granted and at times shutting her out from any real sharing in what he is doing. When Christian husbands do this, giving to Christian activity (which is not necessarily Christian service) a commitment, an interest, and a warm outgoing attentiveness he does not give to his God-given partner, then he sins against God. It is no excuse to say, 'The Lord comes first.' Of course he does, but when he does the husband will love his wife as Christ loved the church. And the husband will not only give thanks to God for his wife, he will also express his love and his gratitude to her.

Parents and children

Read also Exodus 20:1-17

This is quite radical: a call for total, unqualified, unquestioning obedience on the part of children. But it is immediately governed by the equally stringent warning to fathers regarding any unreasonable standards or attitudes. In trying to understand this call to children, and recognizing that our generation is essentially one of rebellion and resentment regarding any kind of discipline, go back to the Ten Commandments which state categorically God's standard for behaviour.

In Exodus 20:12, as the first of the 'manward' commandments and coming before the laws regarding killing, adultery, stealing, lying and coveting, we have the commandment to honour our father and mother, because God's blessing on life is conditional upon it. Note how Paul states that this attitude of glad obedience 'pleases the Lord'. Everything is related to the Lord and it is as we are right with him in our own private persons that we can both be and do right in relationships. Paul has in mind here Christian families, and he would not counsel Christian young people to obey unbelieving parents *'in all things'* because that could lead to direct disobedience to the law of God and call of Christ. But at the same time the child, especially the teenager, must remember the years during which he or she has been provided for and guarded, sometimes at great personal cost to parents. Home life cannot be governed by the wishes, inclinations and demands of children and young people because such wishes are not only self-centred, they also change and are quite unpredictable. But if young people are to respect their parents, then their parents must respect them and not be unreasonable. Talking and listening on both sides helps!

The church family

Read also Proverbs 10:17; 12:1; 22:6

What is being said about the human family applies with equal importance to the spiritual family, the congregation of God's people. Much of the life of churches these days is not only geared to but also governed by the wishes and interests of young people. Such young people may not yet have proved themselves to be truly converted and some of them never do. Youthful enthusiasm for Christ is great to see, but no congregation can be built solely on young people, and one of the most beneficial things for young Christians is that they should learn both duty and obedience, as is made clear in Lamentations 3:25-27.

Children need the influence, stability and example of older people far more than they realize. Young people (especially opinionated Christian young people) need to realize that without the long-continued, often unexciting but faithful service of older people there would not have been congregations for them to be part of. And if there are to be true congregations in the future then children have to learn to grow up humanly and spiritually, and that means taking responsibility. Children are not required to ignore the flaws and limitations of the older generation in human or spiritual things. Older Christians can get stuck in the patterns of the past. It says in Scripture that a little child will lead (Isa. 11:6) and that children can be grown up spiritually in their youth (Ps. 144:12). But the confirmation of spiritual reality, integrity and maturity is that it leads the family of God nearer God and into richer and fuller service. In a real congregation it is not the young, or the old, or any age group in between, that takes precedence. A congregation is a family and has a future when in all areas Christ alone is pre-eminent (Col. 1:18).

Christian parenting

Read also Proverbs 6:20-22; 23:22-26

If children are to honour parents fully then parents must be the kind of people, both humanly and spiritually, who enable and encourage children to do so (Eph. 6:1-4). Children must know and feel that they are loved. This does not mean keeping them smothered emotionally. There are parents (including 'spiritual parents') who never allow their children to grow up and be rightly independent. Some parents hardly allow their children to speak for themselves; always keeping them under close scrutiny, choosing their friends, prescribing their leisure activities, and controlling their Christian activities. Parents can even be cruel by belittling, criticizing and embarrassing their children in front of others. This is different from teasing or cajoling. It is in fact parents manipulating their children, and in some ways trying to live out their own frustrations and ambitions in and through their children. If children are gifted, parents can become obsessed with making them a success, overriding the child's own wishes. If the child is 'ordinary' it can be made to feel inferior and not valued. This is certainly not bringing up children 'by prayer, precept and example, in the nurture and admonition of the Lord' as some of us promised when our children were baptized.

Of course, there must be instruction, correction and discipline, but unless it is consistent and gives the growing young person the right to grow up and to make decisions, there will be rebellion as well as discouragement. Parents must not forget that their growing sons and daughters are no longer little children. They need independence if they are to be their own true persons. It is not easy to let them make decisions when you feel they have got it wrong. But it certainly makes you pray.

Witness at work

Read also Ephesians 6:5-9

The standard set for Christians in the arena of work is not likely to be popular in a generation in which people complain about everything and where personal gain seems to be the main objective in life. Paul's words were not written in an age of unemployment, assembly-line monotony, production quotas and so on, but they were written in a generation of terrible poverty and hardship, and great differences between rich and poor. Slaves had neither rights nor liberties, and therefore revolution, with all the confusion and chaos it brings, was always a real possibility.

Christian slaves were called to be exemplary workers, unquestioned in their loyalty and honesty, and with a heartiness of spirit that could only be maintained by remembering that the 'Master' they really worked for was none other than the Son of God who loved them and gave himself for them. This high standard is set regardless of whether the human master is a believer or not; and it must be recognized that some unbelievers are better and more considerate bosses than believers. Of course, some non-Christians are better workers and better to work with than Christians. A Christian who is a shoddy worker is denying the Lord. A Christian who is difficult to work with is a hindrance to the gospel. The standard of Scripture can cause problems. In many areas work conditions and expectations are increasingly unreasonable and the pressures become almost unbearable. The effect on individuals, marriages and families can be devastating. From time to time, and after much prayerful consideration, it may be the Christian's responsibility to speak up and reason with management for the sake of others, if not for himself. That may result in persecution. But, of course, Jesus was persecuted for doing right.

Right attitudes

Read also Matthew 20:1-16

The attitude to daily work set forth here is so contrary to modern practices that it will help to read other passages on the subject: 1 Timothy 6:1-2; Titus 2:9-10; and 1 Peter 2:18-19. The story Jesus told in Matthew 20:1-16 is not a manifesto for wage settlements but rather a lesson on faithfulness, and a warning against wrong comparisons. Keep in mind also that Paul's letter would be read to the congregation in which believing masters and servants would be worshipping together. It is possible that some believing slave would have grown to such spiritual stature that he would be a teaching and ruling elder, taking spiritual leadership in the church over his week-day master. It is spiritual worth not social or commercial success that qualifies for leadership in the church, and the churches of our day would be in better heart if this had been remembered.

It is a fact of experience that some who are executives in their chosen careers find it very difficult to be just ordinary members of a congregation. When a slave was in a position of spiritual leadership the situation would call for grace on the part of both servant and master, for the one could have pride as well as pleasure in his spiritual position and the other could resent it. That would lead to a wrong spirit in the life of the church and equally so in the work situation. Both slave and master would need to make sure they kept close to the Lord so that there would be no wrong attitudes. In verses 23-24 Paul may be referring to situations where the good slave does not get his due reward and the bad master seems to go free despite his wicked ways. Both slave and master must remember that there is a God who judges and rewards (Rom. 12:17-19). With God there is no favouritism.

Jesus our example

Read also John 13:1-5,12-15

This verse concludes the section on being Christians in daily work. As we seek to witness at work remember that the glorious Son of God took the form of a servant (Phil. 2:6-8) even though he was and is Lord and Master of us all. When Jesus washed the disciples' feet he showed them that humble service was not in any sense a contradiction of his position as their Master. He affirmed that what he did was an example for them and us to follow. All who are masters, having authority over others, must take responsibility for them, leading and directing them by example and not just by word.

Whenever we fail to properly value people, their lives and their feelings, we fall short of all that is meant by leadership. Paul says we must deal justly and fairly, and that means we must be willing to listen to what people say, especially if they are aggrieved. Instead of sweeping away their complaints we must seek to be reasonable and, if we still reject their complaints, we should try to show them why we do so. Leadership and rule over others require us to win their confidence so that they will trust us. Jesus said his sheep would know his voice and follow him. If we look at the wonderful words in 2 Samuel 23:2-4 we will see that right relationships between masters and servants result in blessing for all concerned. Over the whole spectrum of relationships we are to let our Christian light so shine that people will see that the lives we live and the principles we follow flow from what we believe. This is particularly true in the area of daily work. They will give glory to God because they see that being a Christian is what makes all the difference (Matt. 5:13-16).

Prayer

Read also Mark 9:14-29

This exhortation is the culmination of the passage that begins at 3:5 and deals with practical Christian living. Read quickly over the whole passage and see that personal holiness, the harmony of the congregation, the maintaining of true worship, and human relationships have all been dealt with. The standard set is high because the pattern is the character and life of our Lord Jesus Christ. If we are to live like this, then we will most certainly need to be men and women of prayer. Such is the demand, and such will be the volume of our failures, that we will need to hurry to the throne of grace constantly, praying for ourselves, for others and for the work and witness of the church. Praying together also encourages and guards fellowship because in God's presence we need to be both honest and gracious.

Whatever area of life is under pressure, whatever hurts and injustices we have received or feel we have received, before tackling them on the human level we should go to God in prayer. Paul encouraged the Colossians to persevere with this because prayer is what the devil most wants us to neglect. In the face of the great need for missionary evangelism Jesus told his disciples to pray (Matt. 9:36-38). In answer to the powerlessness of the disciples Jesus pointed out their prayerlessness (Mark 9:14-29). When Peter was imprisoned the church prayed earnestly (Acts 12:1-17). It is interesting to note that when Paul was in prison for two years (Acts 24:27) there is no mention of the church at Jerusalem turning to prayer. Perhaps by then the prayer meeting had dwindled away to nothing. It happens again and again. But a congregation whose prayer meeting dies is a congregation which is dying.

Watchfulness

Read also Philippians 4:4-7

The corresponding passage in Ephesians 6:18-20 shows that prayer is at the heart of spiritual warfare. Paul urges perseverance in prayer, aware that the first sign of spiritual declension is the neglect of and distaste for prayer. When he calls for watchfulness he echoes the words of Jesus to his disciples when, at a time of spiritual crisis and significance, they in fact fell asleep (Matt. 26:40-41). We also need to be watchful so that we are always aware of how situations are developing; then prayer will be made right from the beginning and not as a desperate last-ditch stand. This is important in terms of what is happening in the areas of both government and church legislation. It is very important that we should contend for the gospel in the *right places* and on the *right issues*. If we fail to do so we will find all sorts of laws and practices being established which, though appearing innocent at the time, prove in due course to be radical hindrances to the spiritual life of the church.

However, in our prayer life we must not be unduly alarmed or give way to panic because the ultimate outcome of all the issues is in the hand of our sovereign God. This is one reason why our prayers must be joined with thanksgiving. This is sound advice both spiritually and psychologically, because we must never forget blessings already received and future blessings promised. It is God who gives us the victory (1 Cor. 15:57-58) and who *always* leads us along in Christ's triumphal procession (2 Cor. 2:14). Take as a final thought today the words of Paul in Philippians 4:4-7, where prayer, thanksgiving and peace are brought together. When our hearts are at peace we think more clearly, and prayer is seen to be the obvious answer.

Prayer and preaching

Read also Ephesians 6:18-20

These verses teach the importance of prayer in relation to the preaching of the gospel. It is in answer to the prayers of God's people that those called to preach are given utterance (Eph. 6:18-20). By prayer the Word of God speeds on and triumphs (2 Thess. 3:1-2). It is by prayer that the open door of opportunity comes. But prayer must go on, because opportunity does not always mean trouble-free service, as 1 Corinthians 16:9 and 2 Corinthians 2:12-13 make plain. This is why we find Paul writing from prison to the Philippians and linking together their prayers and the working of the Spirit of God for the furtherance of the gospel (Phil. 1:19). God calls men to preach, but preaching is not a 'one man' exercise, and no one person can do all the preaching and all the praying.

Of course, we must remember that Paul was actually in prison as he wrote this epistle (v. 3). But, having appealed to Caesar, he would soon have to state his case for the gospel before the highest court in the Roman empire. A great deal would depend on his presentation of the revealed mystery of Christ, the gospel he was so proud of. He would need much wisdom when he stood before Caesar and his court so that no suspicion would fall on the gospel to hinder the missionary work of the church. There are times of crisis when tremendous care is needed in stating the facts and claims of Christ, lest by undisciplined enthusiasm and unthinking emotion an opportunity is given to the devil. Since Christian truth is always under attack, we must ensure that the cause of the gospel never lacks ongoing, earnest, believing prayer. Pray for those called on to defend the integrity and the message of Scripture, especially in the courts of religious establishment.

Belief and behaviour

Read also Titus 2:1-10

In our day, as in Paul's day, all sorts of stories circulate which denigrate Christians and distort the truth about them. Unfortunately Christians, especially those who are public figures, sometimes say things which are neither wise nor necessary, things so extreme that they are bound to be misunderstood. Some also do things that are morally wrong, things that shock even unbelievers (1 Cor. 5:1-2). This gives an opening to the devil and the work of the gospel is hindered (1 Tim. 6:1). Jesus' counsel was to be wise as serpents and harmless as doves (Matt. 10:16, AV) — not an easy standard.

When Paul calls for wise behaviour in relation to those outside the faith, he was aware that many who never attend church do in fact watch and read the lives of those who claim to be Christians. This is a challenge, but also an opportunity for unselfconscious witness. Just as Jesus could not be hidden (Mark 7:24), so those who walk with Jesus cannot be hidden. Genuine faith, always marked by humility, speaks for itself. On the other hand, false spirituality shouts its presence and grates on people. Paul calls us to 'redeem the time' (v. 5, AV), to make the most of present opportunity, using it to the full while it lasts. Even a passing contact with someone may prove to be a significant moment in their journey to salvation. We must let our light shine, maintain good conduct, live good lives (1 Peter 2:12); do what is right and honourable (2 Cor. 8:21); be manifestly blameless and innocent (Phil. 2:14-15); be sound in speech so that people cannot say anything bad about us (Titus 2:6-8); and be ready to testify to our faith with a clear conscience, knowing that we are concerned only to speak well for Jesus (1 Peter 3:15-16).

A faithful brother

Read also Philippians 2:25-30

We begin here a list of names, which is indicative of the very personal nature of the fellowship in the gospel Paul shared with so many others. Not one of them was taken for granted and Paul was glad to bear testimony to their worth before the whole congregation at Colosse.

Tychicus, the bearer of both this letter and the one to the Ephesians, is seen as Paul's personal envoy. He is the kind of man you miss from a fellowship, a man whose spiritual worth and contribution to the work is realized most when he is no longer there. The description of Tychicus is glorious: a tried and tested brother with a great personal loyalty to Paul, a willing servant and a constant companion right to the end. Read Acts 20:1-5; Titus 3:12; and 2 Timothy 4:12. With regard to this last reference, consider what it must have cost Paul to send away his valued brother at such a trying time, even on the Lord's business. Think also how Tychicus must have felt when saying farewell to Paul, knowing he would not see him again until they met in heaven. Paul describes him as a fellow-servant, bound to Jesus as a willing slave just as he was. Without question this man would encourage the hearts of the believers in Colosse and this is a great and important ministry. Many are able to criticize, correct and even teach. Many tend only to discourage, disturb and demoralize. But happy is the congregation which has within it those who encourage and strengthen hearts in the Lord. This is the spirit that binds people together with a glad willingness to work for Jesus without counting the cost, thinking rather of the *privilege* of being partners together in the gospel (Phil. 1:5,7).

Conversion confirmed

Read also Philemon 1-22

The story of Onesimus, the runaway slave, is in the epistle to Philemon. He had absconded (a serious crime), possibly taking with him goods or money belonging to his master. It seems he sought to get as far away as possible from Colosse (a natural thing for a man on the run) and arrived at Rome. We know nothing of how he came under Paul's ministry and influence. God's ways are past finding out and many a person has been reached and won for Christ far away from home. Perhaps the slave was more open and willing to listen in Rome, possibly with a lingering sense of guilt kindled by the Holy Spirit, whose ways of leading to Christ are varied but perfect. It is clear that the conversion of Onesimus was genuine and he proved himself in his service both with and to Paul. But wrongs done in the past must be put right whenever possible and the time came when it was right to send the runaway back to his master, still a slave but more than a slave, as Philemon 16 declares.

The prospect of returning may have frightened the new believer because technically he could be put to death for his crime. It would also be challenging for his master who had been wronged. But Paul describes Onesimus as 'one of yourselves', reminding both master and congregation that here was a slave, now a Christian, and they must not hold his past against him. With a letter of commendation from Paul the church would be bound to accept Onesimus as a believer in good standing and, if the church accepted him, then his former master could scarcely refuse him. Note the generosity of Paul in Philemon 17-19, and also the reminder that Philemon owed Paul a spiritual debt that could never be repaid.

Two good men

Read also Acts 15:36-41

Aristarchus and Paul had been, in the spiritual sense, fellow prisoners-of-war. They had shared danger and demand together in the service of the gospel (Acts 19:28-34; 20:1-6; 27:1-3). It is clear from these references that Aristarchus was a regular companion of Paul and that he shared in the sea journey and the shipwreck. Then, as some commentators suggest, in Rome he may have actually shared Paul's imprisonment voluntarily, possibly acting as the servant of an important Roman citizen waiting trial. It is good and right to think of this man, and others, alongside Paul, as soldiers of the cross and prisoners of war (Philem. 23; Rom. 16:7; Phil. 2:25).

Mark is the next man mentioned and obviously the Colossians had received some earlier instructions about him. Paul confirms the instructions, making sure Mark would be received properly if he came to Colosse. It may be that some of Mark's history had reached these Christians and they may have had doubts as to his spiritual state and integrity. We have the account relating to Barnabas, Mark and Paul in Acts 15:36-41 when, some twelve years earlier, the young man had opted out of missionary service. Obviously under the guidance of Barnabas, whose name means 'son of encouragement' (Acts 4:36), Mark had proved himself and was reinstated. We find that during Paul's last imprisonment he sent for Mark, bearing testimony to his usefulness (2 Tim. 4:11). Peter also valued Mark (1 Peter 5:13). What a comfort to know that even a great spiritual failure does not disqualify anyone for ever, provided there is true repentance. Evidence of this will be seen in our willingness to learn and return to usefulness in God's service.

An unknown soldier

Read also Romans 9:1-5

Jesus (the Greek form of Joshua) called Justus (his Latin name) is an unknown Christian and all we know about him is what is recorded here. There are many good and faithful Christians whose names never appear on any lists of recognition but their names are in the Lamb's Book of Life (Rev. 21:27). It must have meant a lot to this man to be mentioned by the apostle and to be linked with Mark and Aristarchus. These three were the only Christians of Jewish birth working with Paul at this time in the service of the gospel. They had been a great encouragement to him. Imagine how we would feel if, in a lonely and demanding workplace abroad, we met and built up fellowship with someone from our own homeland who knew our background and used the colloquial expressions that can kindle so many memories.

In Romans 16:7 Paul speaks of other Jews, possibly blood relatives, who had been converted before him. That must have been a great comfort to the man who had such a burdened and sorrowful heart because of the spiritual blindness of his own people, the Jews (Rom. 9:1-5; 10:1-4). If you have prayed long for the conversion of loved ones, take comfort and encouragement from the fact that this great apostle knew that very same burden. If we turn back to the Gospels we will see that our Lord Jesus Christ also knew what it was like to be 'the only one' in the family who was set on doing the will of God (John 7:5). There was a time when his family thought he was mentally and emotionally unbalanced (Mark 3:21). There is no loneliness or hurt or burden that our Saviour cannot understand, feel the pain of, and sympathize with in his full and true humanity.

A church planter

Read also 2 Samuel 23:8,13-17

Paul, like David in the Old Testament, gathered round him a company of mighty men, loving and loyal in their service. We can imagine what it must have been like when such a group gathered together to talk, plan and pray. Epaphras was the missionary evangelist who brought the gospel to Colosse (1:3-8) and he seems to have been the one who planted the churches in Laodicea and Hierapolis. It is not surprising that he was also a great intercessor in the ministry of prayer (v. 12).

The Greek word used to describe Epaphras' prayer could be translated earnest, striving or wrestling in prayer. Here was a minister quite literally sharing in the spiritual battle with and for his converts, praying down upon them the blessing of heaven (cf. Gal. 4:19). His prayers were specific in their objective. He was praying for their increasing spiritual maturity; that they would stand firm in the assurance of the gospel; and that they would ensure they walked right in the centre of God's will for them. Epaphras knew well, in the light of false teaching that proliferated, that shallow conversions and commitment were no use. He prayed that these young Christians would be earnest in their commitment and discipleship. Paul goes on to testify that Epaphras had in every sense been a hard worker in the sphere of ministry. It may have been that the Christians in Colosse had little real understanding of the cost involved in the work, and indeed, they may not have really appreciated the rich ministry they had received. No minister ever wants to make people dependent on him because there is no future in that. But true spiritual growth will never lack genuine expression of gratitude. When the grace of gratitude is lacking something is wrong spiritually.

The beloved doctor

Read also 2 Corinthians 11:23-33

It is only right that a whole reading be devoted to the person, character and work of good and gracious Doctor Luke. How poor we would have been without his Gospel account and the Acts of the Apostles. How much Paul would have missed this gracious man's company, ministry and partnership. There is a possibility that Luke wrote his account of the gospel around the very time Paul was writing to Colosse.

It is interesting that in the Acts narrative Luke, a cultured Greek-speaking Gentile doctor, never obtrudes on the story. He was content to be the personal physician of the great missionary, and who can tell how much he did to preserve Paul's health and strength. In the midst of all his travels he was busy gathering and correlating the facts of Jesus' life and ministry, possibly having no real idea of just how significant his literary labours were. He would not have thought of himself as a man to whom generations of the church would owe a tremendous debt. It was to Luke that Mary opened her heart, giving all the details that mean so much to us at Christmas. It was Luke who travelled with Paul on the fateful journey to Rome (Acts 27:1-8, noting the repetition of 'we'). Acts 28:14 tells us that Luke is there when the company arrived at Rome and then he was separated from Paul. But, at the end of Paul's story, Luke again is with the great man, still ministering to body and spirit (2 Tim. 4:11). When we think not only of Paul's thorn in the flesh (2 Cor. 12:7-9) but also of his physical sufferings (2 Cor. 11:23-28) and his nervous strain and tension (2 Cor. 2:12-13; 7:5), we begin to see what a valuable part the beloved doctor played in Paul's life and work as a missionary.

The backslider

Read also Revelation 2:1-7

We are almost reluctant to turn our attention from Luke, who was such a comfort and encouragement, to Demas who eventually must have been such a heartache to Paul. The fact is recorded for all time in 2 Timothy 4:10 that Demas, in love with the world, deserted both Paul and the work. In Philemon 24 Demas and Luke are referred to as fellow-workers with Paul. Here in Colossians Demas' name is again linked with Luke. But he disappeared from the spiritual scene. Some suggest that he was the kind of man who was carried forward for quite a while by the faith and influence of his friend Luke. It may be that he was on the missionary 'team' on many occasions. He was the kind of man who was associated with and attached to Christian work but was never truly grounded in Christ nor truly committed to his service.

It is a situation that still happens. Some who seem at one stage to be so much part of the spiritual heart of the work lose their warmth, eagerness and participation. They may not be aware of it (Judg. 16:20) and to themselves and others they may deny it. But their hearts have grown cold, even though their theology may still be biblical. They may still be nice, friendly and even helpful in a human way, but spiritually they are neither cold nor hot (Rev. 3:15). In the end they go. They may still attend services, but in their hearts they have strayed. Demas did not just stray. He deserted for love of the world. Just what particular love of the world stole his heart we do not know. It may have been career, or friends, or hobbies, or family, or popularity, or a love affair with a non-believer. Many things can steal the heart. Do not love the world. It is dangerous (1 John 2:15-17; 5:19; Rom. 12:1-2).

A small church

Read also Revelation 3:14-22

Laodicea was about twelve miles north-west of Colosse, and Nympha was one of the believers. It is interesting that it is a woman who is named although 'brothers' are referred to. The church was apparently meeting in her house. This may throw light on the letter to Laodicea in Revelation 3:14-22, suggesting that the main congregation had fallen into spiritual complacency and carelessness, but there seems to have been a remnant of faith standing firm and meeting in Nympha's house. Perhaps that little group was considered by the others as being extreme, exclusive and schismatic. That can indeed happen, and has resulted on some occasions in our own day in so-called 'house churches'. On the other hand, there may be an indication here that in many places the early church congregations were small in number and yet they were the recipients of Paul's letters, care and attention, just as much as the larger congregations. We all tend to be unduly influenced for encouragement or discouragement by numbers and statistics.

Another lesson we can learn from these simple verses is to think of small groups of believers maintaining worship and witness in the midst of a pagan society; sharing fellowship with one another and encouraging each other in the faith. This is something we ourselves may well have to do increasingly, as our own society becomes more and more godless and profane. We need each other, and we need the refreshing and reviving 'air' of fellowship and worship, just as we need the ministry of God's Word as the bread of our souls. Make a point today of praying for those who week after week have little or nothing of either fellowship or ministry.

Be faithful

Read also Acts 20:17-24

No one is sure who Archippus was, but it is suggested that he may have been a member of the family of Philemon (Philem. 2) or at least a member of that household. Paul called on him publicly (because this letter would be read to the gathered church) to see to it that he carried out to the full the ministry he had been called to. Just what that ministry was is not stated, although it could be the ministry of the Word. No doubt some of the mature members of the church in Colosse would see the need for Paul's challenge. Perhaps Archippus was easing off in his dedication and work, or he may have allowed himself to be involved in so many aspects of Christian work that he was failing to carry out properly the task God had really called him to. If you are called to preach make sure that thorough preparation is given to every sermon. This public attention upon the man must have been painful for him, but it was the kind of challenge that would either make or break him.

No true pastor of God's people can stand back and allow a gifted person to waste his talents on secondary service. Paul was simply saying to Archippus, and to all of us, to take heed, to be on the watch, because it is so easy to let things slip and to be less than the Lord calls us to be. This slipping or falling short can arise even when we ourselves think we are doing well, and when others may be admiring and praising us. But there is no value in self-praise (Rom. 12:3; 2 Cor. 10:12), or in the praise of others, if God is grieved with us because we are not fulfilling the ministry to which he has called us and for which he has equipped us. Note carefully the words spoken to the church in Revelation 2:1-5; 3:1-3,15-17. See to it that God is pleased with you.

The signature

Read also Philippians 4:10-14

As was his custom, Paul wrote the last few words and signature in his own handwriting (cf. 1 Cor. 16:21-24; 2 Thess. 3:17-18). In Galatians 6:11 the reference to writing in large letters may suggest that Paul's eyesight was failing or it may signify how difficult and painful it was for him to take the pen in his sore, twisted fingers: an indication of how much he had suffered physically in his service of the gospel.

In 2 Thessalonians 2:1-2 we see that there were forged letters, purporting to come from Paul. This should help us to be alert to distortions of the Christian message in newspaper advertisements and spoken by people knocking at our doors. But the emphasis of this last verse is really on the humanity of the great apostle. As he took the pen he was aware of the weight of the chains on his hands. He was a prisoner for Jesus' sake. Although he rejoiced and had learned to be content (Phil. 1:12; 4:11-13), he was still intensely human, and he expresses deep feeling when he asks them to remember his chains. It is all too easy to forget that the great servants of God may be spiritual giants, but they are not immune to physical, mental and emotional pain. They will not make a show of it lest they distract attention away from Christ and the gospel. But on occasions, almost on impulse as it seems here, they open their hearts and say, 'We need your care and your prayers.' We can but hope that some in Colosse made it their business to write to Paul, not least to assure him of prayer. All of us have the opportunity to encourage others. There were times when Paul felt forgotten, and needed someone, as Jesus did, to watch with him. Picture Paul, having written the words, raising his hands in benediction, saying, 'Grace be with you.'

Notes

Philippians

1. J. I. Packer, *Knowing God*, Hodder & Stoughton.
2. Prayer by Reinhold Niebuhr (1892-1971), quoted in the *Lion Prayer Collection*, Lion Publications, 1992.
3. From the hymn 'Our blest Redeemer, ere He breathed' by Henriette Auber (1773-1862).
4. Norman Grubb, *C. T. Studd, Cricketer and Pioneer*, Lutterworth Press, UK, 1933.
5. From the hymn by Katie B. Wilkinson (1859-1928).
6. From the hymn 'See amid the winter's snow' by E. Caswall (1814-78).
7. From the hymn 'Once in royal David's city' by C. F. Alexander (1823-95).
8. From the hymn 'Hark the herald angels sing', by Charles Wesley (1707-88).
9. 'Just as I am' by Charlotte Elliott (1789-1871).
10. From the hymn 'And can it be?' by Charles Wesley (1707-88).
11. J. B. Phillips, *Translation of New Testament*.
12. From the hymn 'Praise the Saviour, ye who know Him!' by Thomas Kelly (1769-1855).
13. 'Be still my soul' by Catharina von Schlegel (b. 1697).
14. From the poem 'Tam o' Shanter' by Robert Burns.
15. From the hymn 'What a friend we have in Jesus' by Joseph Scriven (1819-86).
16. O. Hallesby, *Prayer*, IVP.
17. From the hymn 'O Thou by whom we come to God', by James Montgomery (1771-1855).

18. From the hymn 'Peace, perfect peace' by Edward H. Bickersteth (1825-1906).
19. From the hymn 'Rescue the perishing' by Fanny Crosby (1823-1915).

Colossians

1. John Calvin, *Calvin Commentary on Galatians, Ephesians, Philippians and Colossians*, St Andrew Press (1965), p.298.
2. From the hymn 'Dear Lord and Father of mankind', by John Greeleaf Whittier (1807-92).
3. From the hymn 'Our Lord Christ hath risen' by William Conyngham Plunket (1828-97), Church Hymnary Revised Edition, Oxford University Press, 1927.
4. From the hymn 'When I survey the wondrous cross' by Isaac Watts (1674-1748).
5. From the hymn 'Hark the herald angels sing' by Charles Wesley (1707-88).
6. William Shakespeare, *Hamlet*, Act 5, scene 2, line 10.
7. From the hymn 'Go labour on' by Horatius Bonar (1808-89).
8. From 'A debtor to mercy alone' by Augustus Toplady (1740-78).
9. *Scottish Paraphrases* 48, 'The Saviour died but rose again'.
10. From the hymn 'Love divine, all loves excelling' by Charles Wesley (1707-88).
11. From the poem 'Tam o' Shanter' by Robert Burns.
12. Albert Orsborn, *Songs of victory*, Salvationist Publishing.
13. Moffat, *Translation of the New Testament*, 1 Corinthians 13.
14. Handley C. G. Moule, *Colossian and Philemon studies*, Pickering and Inglis, London & Glasgow, p.222.

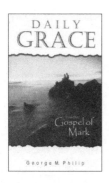

Daily grace is a collection of daily meditations, which takes the reader through the whole of the Gospel of Mark. The readings are straightforward, yet imaginative and thought-provoking, emphasizing both the sovereignty of God and Christ's real humanity in all the events surrounding the Lord's life on earth.

Each meditation is helpfully confined to a page's length, and includes further readings for supplementary study. With concise and clear exposition, the author sets the scene for each encounter with Christ as recorded by Mark and his contemporary style takes us through the Gospel at an exciting and stimulating pace.

Ideal for personal study, the readings are also helpful for Bible class preparation and to inspire pastors and teachers who wish to study and preach from the Gospel of Mark.

'While these notes have been produced over many years for congregational daily readings, they have been widely used by preachers also — with immense benefit and profit.'
                                        David C. Searle, Rutherford House

Daily grace from the Gospel of Mark, George M. Philip, Evangelical Press/Rutherford House, 192 pages, ISBN 0 85234 468 6.